tommy walsh
LIVINGSPACES DIY

tommy walsh
LIVINGSPACESDIY

Collins

To my wife Marie and my kids, Charlotte, Natalie and Jonjo, for putting up with my manic lifestyle, and the fact that on the rare occasions that I am home, I'm often secreted away in my study writing.

First published in 2004 by Collins an imprint of HarperCollins*Publishers*, 77-85 Fulham Palace Road, London, W6 8JB

The Collins website address is: www.**collins**.co.uk

Text copyright © Tommy Walsh
Photography, artworks and design © HarperCollins*Publishers*

Designed and produced by Airedale Publishing Ltd
Art Director: Ruth Prentice
PA to Art Director: Amanda Jensen
Editors: Jackie Matthews, Carole McGlynn
Designer: Hannah Attwell
Assistants: Andres Arteaga, Anthony Mellor, Neal Kirby
DTP: Max Newton, Antony Cairns
Tommy Walsh photographs: David Murphy
Other photographs: Sarah Cuttle, Mike Newton, David Murphy
Artworks: David Ashby
Consultant: John McGowan
Index: Emma Callery

For HarperCollins
Senior Managing Editor: Angela Newton
Editor: Alastair Laing
Design Manager: Luke Griffin
Editorial Assistant: Lisa John
Production Controller: Chris Gurney

A CIP catalogue record for this book is available from the British Library

ISBN: 0007156863
Colour reproduction: Colourscan
Printed and bound: Lego, Italy

1 living spaces basics 13

3 living spaces downstairs 73

contents

living spaces
planning 53

living spaces
upstairs 97

introduction

The kitchen and bathroom are generally considered to be the two most expensive areas of the home to refurbish and a separate book is dedicated to each of these rooms. This leaves what I've collectively termed 'living space', encompassing the rest of the home. This space starts at the front door and extends to the bedrooms, including the living room, dining room, hallway, staircase and landing – all the important spaces within our homes.

This book addresses how to deal with these spaces, in terms of planning, and takes you step by step through the provision of basic electricity, light fittings and central heating as well as decorating – painting and wallpapering – and building in extras such as shelving, wardrobes and window seats. Advice is given on adapting spaces where necessary and handy tips on regular maintenance will help you to get the best from all your rooms.

There is an ongoing debate about whether refurbishing your home increases its value. I believe this will inevitably happen, provided the quality of the work is of a high standard. Improving your home is all about making it work for you, thereby creating a happier environment for the whole family for the duration of the time you live there.

So plan well, take your time and enjoy the results of your hard labour – just as I do!

tools

Power tools, although useful for a variety of jobs, need to be employed with care and should be complemented by a good selection of hand tools. The tools you need for the projects in this book will be used time and time again, so ensure that they are of a good quality, fit comfortably in your hand, and feel right! Build up your collection of tools carefully, always clean them thoroughly and store them away after use. Most importantly, don't loan them out to anybody – experience has shown me that, on the odd occasion the tools are returned, they are rarely in the pristine condition they were before being loaned out!

LARGE TOOLS & DRILLS

always read the safety information provided BEFORE use and practise before using a tool for the first time

1 toolbox
2 14 volt cordless drill
3 18 volt cordless drill
4 cordless hammer drill

5 small cordless drill
6 drillbit selection
7 corded jigsaw
8 radial arm mitre saw (right)

GENERAL TOOLS

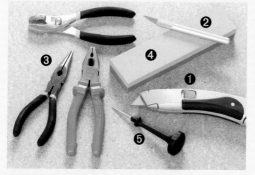

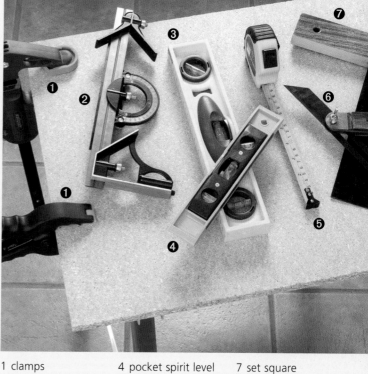

1 large craft knife   4 oilstone
2 small craft knife   5 bradawl
3 pliers & pincers

1 clamps   4 pocket spirit level   7 set square
2 adjustable square   5 tape measure
3 spirit level   6 sliding bevel

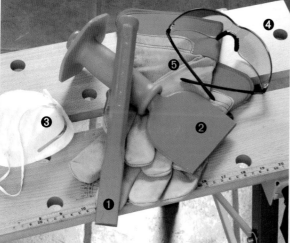

safety glasses
and a mask are
essential for any
task that could
produce flying
pieces

1 cold chisel   4 safety glasses
2 bolster chisel   5 gloves
3 dust mask

GENERAL TOOLS

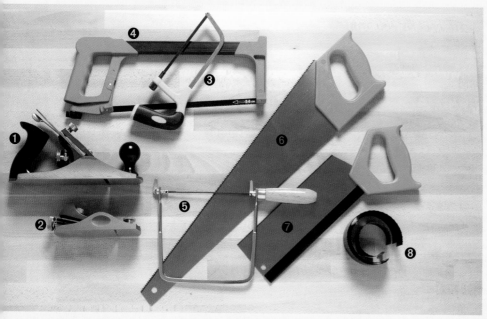

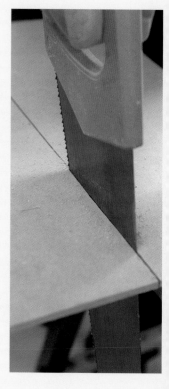

1 wood plane
2 block plane
3 hack saw (junior)

4 large hacksaw
5 coping saw
6 hand saw

7 tenon saw
8 set of hole saws

1 claw hammer
2 chisel selection
3 screwdriver selection
4 rubber mallet
5 pin hammer

ELECTRICAL TOOLS

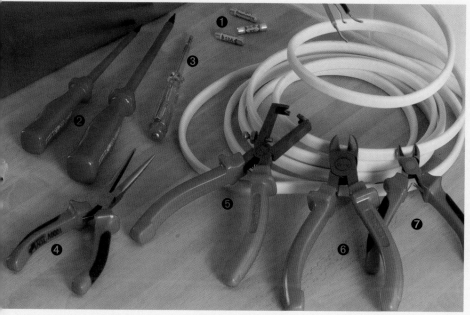

1 fuses
2 electric screwdrivers
3 tester screwdriver
4 long nose pliers
5 wire strippers
6 cable cutters
7 wire cutters
8 electrical tester
(above right)

PLUMBING TOOLS

1 adjustable spanners
2 gas torch & fire-proof mat
3 plier wrench
4 copper pipe cutter
5 PTFE tape
6 replacement fittings

WALLPAPERING TOOLS

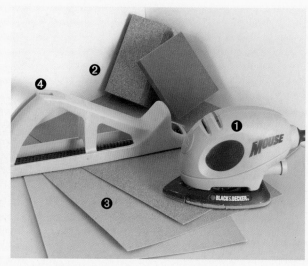

1 wallpaper shears
2 wallpaper brush
3 pasting brush
4 scraper
5 pasting table

DECORATING TOOLS

1 palm sander
2 sanding blocks
3 sandpaper
4 sander

PAINTING TOOLS

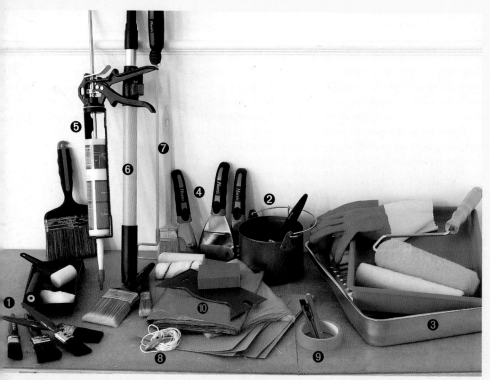

1 paintbrushes
2 paint kettle
3 roller & paint tray
4 filling knives
5 sealant gun
6 roller extension pole
7 flexible roller and radiator brush
8 plumb line
9 masking tape and knife
10 paint mask and plastic dust sheets

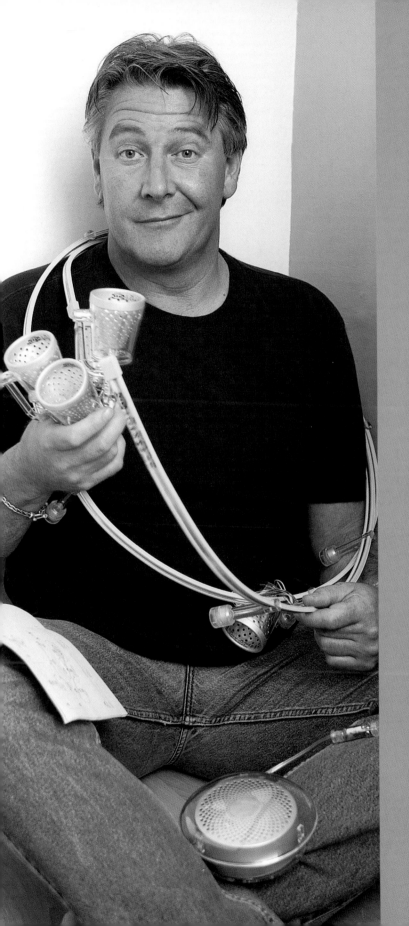

living spaces

basics

Just like starting to cook by boiling an egg, let's go back to basics! Regular DIY maintenance of the interior fabric of your home will, in the long run, save you money and avoid tempers raised over the cost of tradesmen and builders.

basic electrics

We tend to take our electricity supply for granted – after all, it's always available at the flick of a switch! However, it's important to understand how electricity works in your home, in case anything should go wrong or you want to carry out some simple improvements. If you are unsure about an electrical job, though, it's always best to call in an electrician.

HOW IT WORKS

Electricity travels from your local electricity sub-station to your house via the live, or phase, conductor of the supply cable. This connects directly to a central distribution unit, which controls the electricity circuits to the various parts of your home. The current flows through the individual circuits providing power for lighting and appliances, before it returns to the sub-station via the neutral conductor of the supply cable.

THE CONSUMER UNIT

In an old or unmodernized house, the distribution unit is known as a fuse board or fuse box. This has a main on–off switch to control the whole system, and one or more panels (fuse boxes) containing wire fuses that protect the

individual light and power circuits. Modern wiring systems have a one-piece control centre known as a consumer unit **1**. This combines the main on–off switch and the protection for each circuit in one neat enclosure. The individual circuits may be protected by wire or cartridge fuses, like an old fuse box, or instead by small switches called miniature circuit breakers (MCBs) **2**. The fuses or MCBs have a current rating to match the likely demand of the circuit they are protecting – 5 or 6 amps for lighting circuits, 30 or 32 amps for circuits to socket outlets, perhaps a 15-amp circuit to an immersion heater, and a 45-amp circuit to a cooker or electric shower. Each fuse or switch should be labelled to remind you which circuit it belongs to.

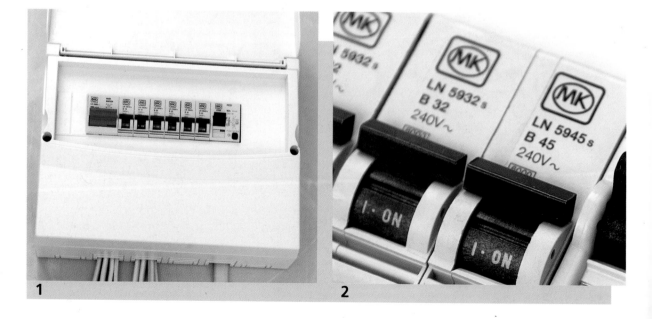

1

2

ELECTRICAL SAFETY

The purpose of a fuse or MCB is to protect the circuit cable from being overloaded. If you try to draw more current than the circuit was designed to supply – for example, by plugging in too many high-wattage appliances – the cable will overheat. On an unprotected circuit this could easily start a fire. To prevent this happening, a wire fuse will melt and stop the current flow, while an MCB will turn off automatically. You have to repair or replace a fuse to restore the supply, but with an MCB you simply turn it back on again. That's after you've unplugged the offending appliance, of course!

3

Some consumer units contain an additional – and in my view essential – form of protection known as a residual current device (RCD) **3**. This immediately detects any current leakage, which can happen if the insulation on a circuit cable fails, or if you touch something live and the current flows through your body, and switches off the supply in a fraction of a second – fast enough to save your life! It usually protects only certain circuits in the house – mainly those supplying socket outlets. If a fault occurs and the RCD switches off, you cannot switch it on again until the fault has been discovered and put right.

The other important safety feature of your wiring system is earthing. This literally means a connection to the earth, and it provides an escape route for current that leaks from the system because of an electrical fault or due to you touching something that is live. Each circuit cable contains an earth conductor that is connected to a main earth terminal at your fuse board or consumer unit. It is vital that this conductor is continuous throughout each circuit and is connected to each lighting point, socket outlet or free-standing appliance.

4

To provide additional protection, exposed metalwork such as plumbing pipes and metal kitchen sinks are also connected to the earthing system. This means that should the metalwork become live due to inadvertent contact with any part of the wiring system, the current would be earthed, so that you would not receive a shock if you touched it! Look out for special metal earth tags on pipes and other metalwork, each connected to a green-and-yellow sheathed earth cable **4**, and make sure you never disconnect these cables.

SWITCHING OFF

Always switch off the power supply when carrying out any electrical repairs or improvements. If you have circuit fuses, turn off the main on–off switch and then remove the fuseholder protecting the circuit you want to work on. You can then turn the switch on again to restore the supply to the other circuits. If you have a consumer unit with MCBs, simply switch off the relevant circuit MCB.

RING MAIN CIRCUITS

We all know that most electrical appliances get their power by being plugged into a wall-mounted socket outlet. What we might not realize is that each socket is connected to a ring main circuit, a cable that runs in a ring around the rooms it serves. Both ends of the circuit cable are connected to the live and neutral terminals in the house fuse board or consumer unit (see page 14). As the current can flow to a socket outlet either way round the ring, the circuit's capacity is capable of serving any number of socket outlets, which may be single, double or triple types.

> ## always switch off the power supply when carrying out any electrical repairs or improvements

The only restriction on a ring main circuit is the total floor area of the rooms it serves – a maximum of 100 sq m (1075 sq ft). The average modern home has lots of low-wattage technology around that is not all switched on at the same time. This means that most homes have two or three ring main circuits – often one for upstairs rooms and one for downstairs, plus a separate ring for the kitchen, where most appliances are used.

The ring main circuit can also supply socket outlets connected to it by a spur cable – a sort of branch line that is connected to the ring main circuit either at a socket outlet on the circuit **1**, or at a special junction box **2**. The circuit can supply as many spurs as there are socket outlets on the ring main circuit itself. This allows you to add extra socket outlets to the circuit if you wish.

REPLACING A SOCKET OUTLET

Most socket outlets in the home, whether fixed on to the wall surface or flush-mounted (inset), have a white plastic faceplate, but more attractive metallic, coloured plastic and wooden finishes are also available. If you want to change a faceplate as part of a room makeover, it is a simple job to unscrew and disconnect the old faceplate and fit a new one.

Turn off the power to the circuit supplying the socket outlet you want to work on (see page 15). Plug in and switch on an appliance to check that the power is off. On a flush-mounted socket outlet, cut round the back edge of the faceplate using a sharp knife to break the seal formed by painting the wall **3**. Remove the two faceplate fixing screws **4** and carefully ease the faceplate away from the mounting box. Make a note of how many cables are present, and which cable conductors go to which terminal. According to the status of the socket outlet there may be one cable (on a spur), two (on the ring main circuit) or three (on the circuit and supplying a spur). Loosen the terminal screws and pull out the cable

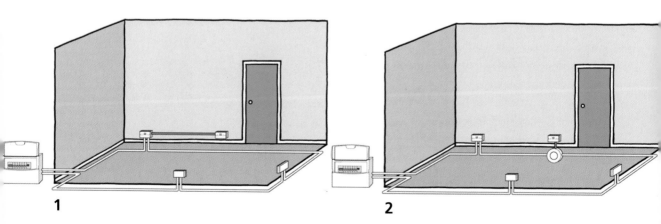

1   **2**

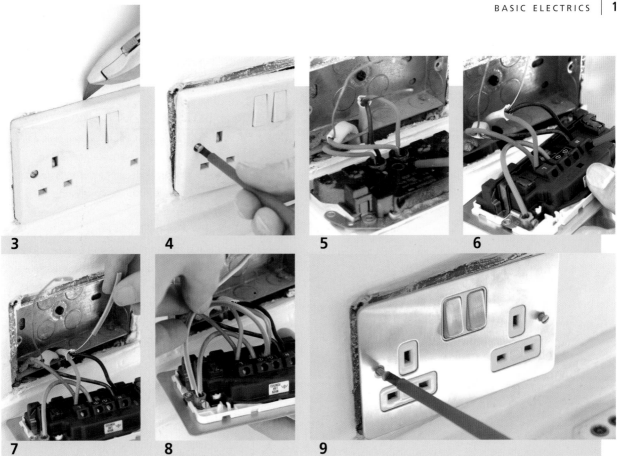

3
4
5
6
7
8
9

conductors (called cores) **5**. Set aside the old faceplate and fixing screws.

Connect the cores to the terminals on the back of the new faceplate. Connect the red core (or cores if there is more than one cable present) to the terminal marked L or live, and the black core (or cores) to the terminal marked N or neutral **6**.

The third core in each cable is the earth core. This bare copper wire must be covered with a piece of green-and-yellow PVC earth sleeving before being connected to the earth terminal on the faceplate. If you find the cores in your socket outlet are bare, buy some sleeving and cut pieces to fit each bare earth core **7**.

If you are fitting a metal faceplate on to a flush metal mounting box, you must fit an earth link between the earth terminal on the faceplate and the one in the box. Use a short length of earth conductor from a cable offcut, and cover it with PVC sleeving before fitting it **8**. Double-check that all the cores are securely held in their terminals.

Then carefully fold the cables back into the mounting box and screw the new faceplate to it **9**. Restore the power supply to the circuit and test the new socket outlet.

👍 **TOP TIP Keep the fixing screws from the old faceplate in case you need them for the new one. Old mounting boxes may have imperial threads in their fixing lugs, and the metric screws supplied with the new faceplate may not engage in the old lugs.**

TOMMY'S WARNING

I remember when I was very young changing a damaged low-level single power socket in our kitchen while my Dad was at work. Unfortunately, I didn't know that the power had to be turned off. Amazingly, I survived even though I received a couple of stiff shocks, which has given me a lifelong respect for electricity. **So remember – always switch off and, if in doubt, switch off the entire supply to the house.**

LIGHTING CIRCUITS

Your home will probably have two lighting circuits – one for upstairs rooms and one for downstairs. Each one will be protected by a circuit fuse or MCB rated at 5 or 6 amps (see page 14). Ceiling lights are connected to the circuit cables, which run within the ceiling voids. Wall lights are supplied by cables running in channels cut in the wall plaster, or concealed within timber-framed partition walls.

Unlike a ring main circuit (see page 16), a lighting circuit is a single track. It starts at the fuse board or consumer unit and runs from one lighting point to the next, terminating at the most remote light on the circuit. On a modern system, the cable runs directly into each ceiling rose or light fitting and out again to the next light – a system called loop-in wiring. The cable to the switch that controls the light is also connected at the ceiling rose or the light fitting.

LOOP-IN SYSTEM

If you unscrew the cover of a loop-in ceiling rose (after switching off the supply, of course) you will find three sets of terminals. There will be three cables present (or just two if it is the final light on the circuit). Two are the circuit cables, the third the switch cable. The flex to a pendant lampholder is also wired into the terminals.

JUNCTION BOX SYSTEM

Older lighting circuits use junction boxes containing four terminals, rather than loop-in roses. A junction box is wired into the circuit cable near each lighting point, and separate cables run from the box to the ceiling rose or light fitting and to its switch. There are four cables in all the boxes, except in the one at the last lighting point on the circuit, which has three cables. If you unscrew a ceiling rose on a junction-box system, you will find just one cable present.

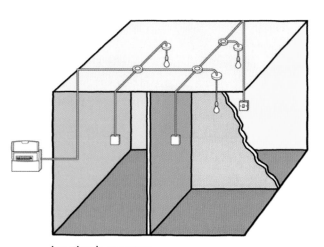

junction box system

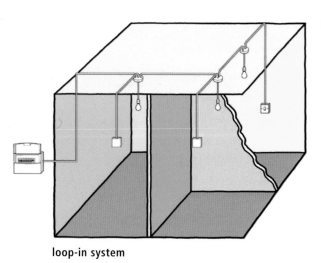

loop-in system

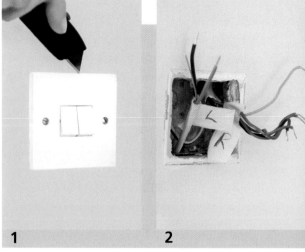

1   **2**

REPLACING A LIGHT SWITCH

As with socket outlets (see page 16), you might want to replace an old light switch as part of a room makeover. The job is even simpler than replacing a socket outlet because there is usually only one cable present. Turn off the power to the circuit supplying the light (see page 15), then switch the light on to check that the power is off.

Cut around, unscrew and ease away the old faceplate **1**, as described on page 16. If the switch is part of a two-way switching arrangement, such as in a hall or landing, the two switches will be linked with special three-core-and-earth cable. Note which core – red, yellow and blue – goes to which terminal. A two-way switch (which is wired to another switch) allows a light to be controlled from either switch, and has three terminals on the back of the faceplate; make sure you buy a similar replacement.

A two-gang switch, which has two rocker switches, controls two lights from one faceplate, and there will be cables going to each half of the switch. Label these Left and Right, so you don't muddle them up later on **2**. Disconnect the cable cores from their terminals.

With two-way switches, connect the three-core cable to the three terminals, copying the arrangement you noted **3**. With one-way switches, connect the red and black cores to the new faceplate terminals as in the old switch **4**.

If the old faceplate was plastic, the cable earth core will be connected to an earth terminal in the mounting box only. If you are fitting a new metal faceplate to a metal mounting box, you must add an earth link between the faceplate and box **5** (see also page 17). Use a short length of earth conductor from a cable offcut, and cover it with a piece of green-and-yellow PVC earth sleeving. Double-check that the cores are securely held in their terminals, then carefully fold the cables back into the mounting box and screw on the faceplate **6**. Restore the power supply and test the new switch.

👍 **TOP TIP Remember that it's advantageous to tackle this job at the weekend during daylight for obvious reasons!**

FITTING A DIMMER SWITCH

You can replace an existing light switch with a dimmer switch, as long as it is not controlling a fluorescent light. Choose a dimmer switch that will fit the existing mounting box; some require a deeper-than-normal box. Check, too, that the wattage of the lights being controlled is within the stated wattage range of the dimmer switch.

Turn off the power to the lighting circuit (see page 15), then unscrew the faceplate of the existing switch and disconnect the cable cores. Connect the cable cores to the new dimmer switch faceplate, following the manufacturer's wiring instructions. Screw the new faceplate to the mounting box and restore the power supply.

3

4

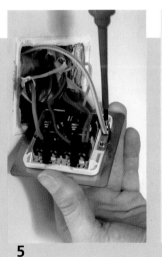

5

6

installing new light fittings

New light fittings can change the look of a room dramatically, especially if all you have at present is a central light fitting with a rose, a pendant lampholder and a lampshade. There is a vast range of fittings available in lighting, home furnishing and DIY stores, ranging from traditional chandeliers to ultra-modern track and spotlight fittings.

TYPES OF FITTING

Installing a new fitting is not difficult, but it is essential that you understand how the existing wiring is connected and how to modify it to supply your new fitting. Try and design the lighting to suit your needs, producing the required amount of light and not just desirable-looking fittings! As soon as you decide you want to install a new light fitting, take a little time to examine the existing wiring at the lighting point you want to change. Before you start, remember to turn off the power to the lighting circuit (see page 15) then test that there is no power by turning on the light switch.

If you have a ceiling rose, you can simply unscrew its cover to reveal the baseplate. You may need to use a sharp knife to cut through old paint sticking the rose cover to the ceiling surface. If only one cable is present, this can be disconnected then reconnected directly to the terminal block or flex tail of your new light fitting. Two or three cables present means you have loop-in wiring (see page 18), with the light switch cable connected in at the rose. You will have to replicate this wiring when you connect the new light fitting. As this will require the use of a strip of four small terminal blocks, which measures 30 x 20 x 15mm (1¼ x ¾ x ⅝in), make sure you choose a light fitting with enough room inside its baseplate to accommodate the strip.

Where a light fitting is already installed, unscrew or otherwise remove its cover. This should reveal either a terminal block attached to the fitting, or a strip of terminal blocks used to connect the circuit cable(s) to a flex tail emerging from the fitting. In either case, it will be a simple job to unscrew and disconnect the existing fitting, and to reconnect the wiring to the new one.

NEW FIXINGS

You will need to look at your new light fitting to see how it should be attached to the ceiling. If the fixing holes are close together, you should be able to screw it directly to the ceiling joist above the old rose baseplate. If they are more than about 75mm (3in) apart, you may still be able to screw the fitting to the joist. You can make some test drillings to locate it precisely. Otherwise you may have to use cavity fixings (spring toggles, for example) to secure the fitting to the ceiling.

DISCONNECTING A CEILING ROSE

With the power off and the ceiling rose cover removed, double-check that the power is off with a tester **1**. Disconnect the pendant's flex cores from their terminals

1

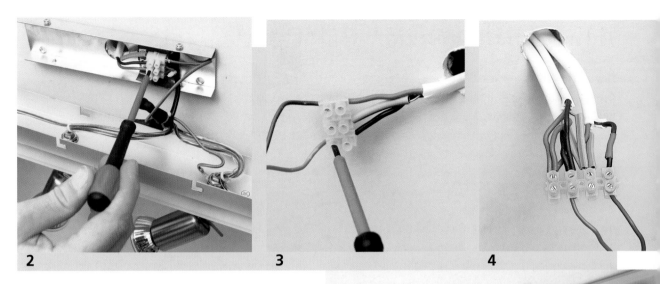

2   3   4

and discard the pendant. If there is more than one cable present, make a note of which cable cores are connected to which terminals. You should find all the live (red) cores connected to the centre terminal on the rose baseplate. The neutral (black) cores of the incoming and outgoing circuit cables will be connected to one end terminal, and the black (switch return) core of the switch cable will be connected to the other end terminal. Mark the cable sheaths for identification (see page 18) and disconnect all the cores from their terminals. Unscrew the baseplate from the ceiling and set it aside.

CONNECTING THE NEW FITTING

You have to make the electrical connections before mounting the new fitting on the ceiling. Make sure that you support it as you work so no strain is imposed on the connections.

If only one circuit cable is present and the new fitting has a fixed terminal block, connect the red core to the terminal marked L, the black core to the terminal marked N and the green-and-yellow sleeved earth core to the terminal marked E **2**.

If only one cable is present and the new fitting has two flex tails, use a strip of three terminal blocks to connect cable to flex. Link the red cable core to the brown flex core, the black cable core to the blue flex core and the sleeved cable earth core into the middle terminal **3**.

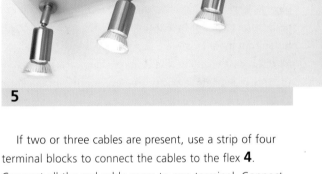

5

If two or three cables are present, use a strip of four terminal blocks to connect the cables to the flex **4**. Connect all the red cable cores to one terminal. Connect the circuit cable black cores and the flex blue core to the second terminal. Connect the cable earth cores to the third terminal. Connect the switch cable black core (which may be identified with some red PVC tape) and the flex brown core to the fourth terminal.

MOUNTING THE NEW FITTING

Once you have completed the connections to the new fitting, tuck the strip of terminal blocks inside its baseplate. Offer up the baseplate to the ceiling and fix it in place. Screw it to the joist if possible. Otherwise drill clearance holes for cavity fixings, insert these and tighten the fixing screws. Restore the power supply and test the new light **5**.

LOW-VOLTAGE LIGHTING

Low-voltage lighting is supplied with power at 12 volts
from a transformer. This means that power consumption is
greatly reduced compared with mains lighting at 240 volts.
The other advantage is that the fittings use small halogen
bulbs, which give an intense white light that is perfect for
creating dramatic lighting effects or highlighting features
of the room. Halogen bulbs are more expensive than
standard light bulbs, but have a relatively long life provided
that they are not repeatedly switched on and off (so, in
other words, you may have to get used to sleeping with
the lights on!).

CHOOSING FITTINGS

There are three main types of low-voltage light fitting.
The first is designed as a direct replacement for an existing
light fitting. It consists of a round, surface-mounted base
unit, which contains the transformer, and a circular plate, a
rigid bar or a twin-wire track on which the individual light
fittings are mounted. The halogen bulbs are usually rated
at 20 watts.

    The second type consists of a separate transformer,
which has to be concealed in the ceiling void (see page
24), and a number of individual low-voltage fittings
(usually recessed downlighters), which are connected to
the transformer by lengths of cable. The transformer
wattage is matched to the total wattage of the lamps it is
supplying. These may be rated at 20 or 50 watts.

    The third type consists of individual light fittings (again,
usually downlighters), each with its own slimline
transformer (see page 25). These fittings are wired in series,
and each transformer is designed so it can be passed up into
the ceiling void through the hole cut for the fitting. Access
is needed to the ceiling void to install the cable run from
light to light. Again, 20- or 50-watt bulbs are usually fitted.

SURFACE-MOUNTED FITTINGS

Turn off the power. If you are replacing an existing ceiling
rose or light fitting, site the new fitting so the transformer
unit is mounted over the old light position **1**. The existing

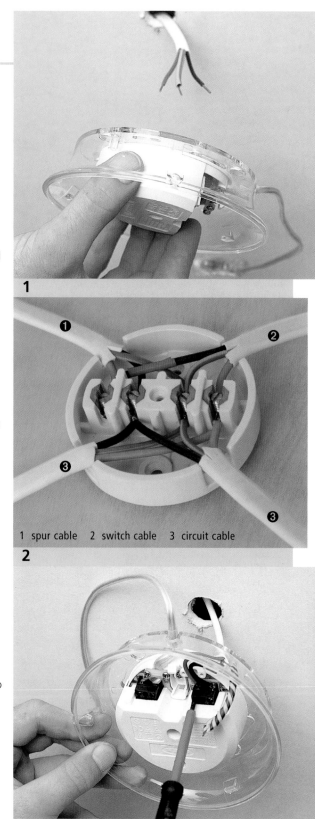

1 spur cable   2 switch cable   3 circuit cable

wiring can then be connected directly to the transformer terminals. If the fitting is to be installed in a new position, run a spur cable to it, via access from the ceiling cavity, from the lighting circuit, to a new four-terminal junction box wired into the circuit **2**. You can then connect a switch cable to the junction box to provide separate control of the new light.

Disconnect and remove the existing ceiling rose or light fitting (see pages 20–21). If only one cable is present, connect it to the transformer input terminals. The transformer does not need earthing, so cut off the cable earth core flush with the cable sheath, or wrap it in PVC insulating tape for future re-use if the light fitting is changed again **3**.

If two or three cables are present, connect them to a strip of four terminal blocks, as described on pages 20–21. Then connect one end of a short length of cable to the switch return and neutral terminal blocks in the strip, and the other end to the transformer input terminals **4**. Pull the bare earth core out of the cable sheath before connecting this cable up; it is not needed.

Screw the transformer unit to the ceiling – directly to a joist if possible, or with cavity fixings otherwise. If it has a track or support wires, attach the mounting brackets to the ceiling and fit the bar or wires into them. Position the light fittings as required and restore the power supply **5**.

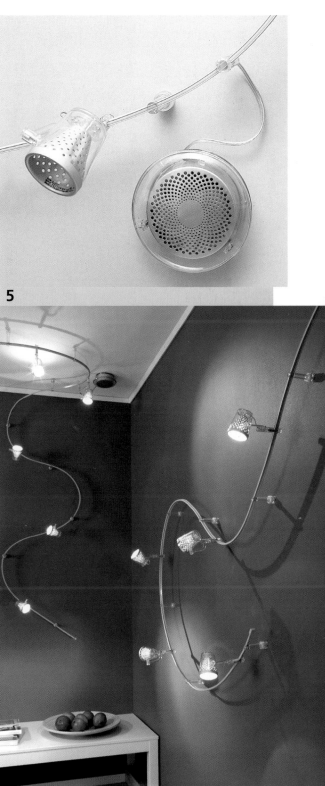

5

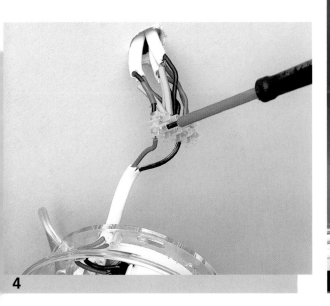

4

transformers greatly reduce the consumption of power

1

2

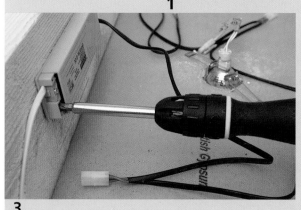

3

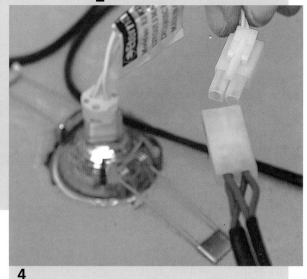

4

SINGLE-TRANSFORMER SYSTEMS

Turn off the power and gain access to the ceiling void above where the lights are to be installed. Run the power supply to the transformer as a spur from a new four-terminal junction box into which the new switch cable is also wired. See Surface-mounted fittings (page 22) for the wiring diagram.

Cut a hole in the ceiling at each light position, using a hole saw **1**. Clip the fitting into the hole **2**. Screw the transformer to the side of a joist **3** and connect the supply cable to its input terminals. Run a feed cable from the transformer output terminals to each light position **4** and connect each feed cable to its terminal block. Clip the cable to the side of the nearest joist. Run cable from the junction box to the position of the new light switch. Mount this and connect the cable to it. Restore the power supply and test the new lights **5**.

5

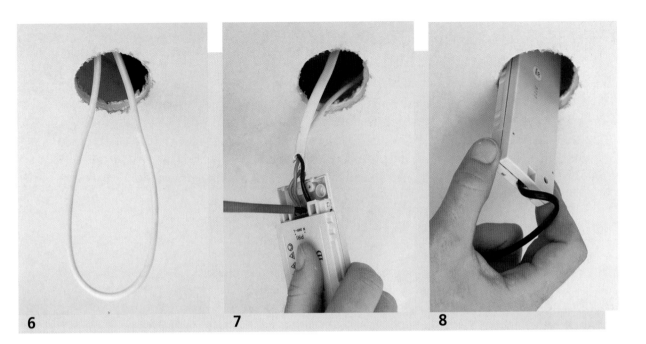

6 **7** **8**

MULTI-TRANSFORMER SYSTEMS

This is similar in wiring terms to the single transformer system described opposite, except that every light has its own transformer in the ceiling. The circuit cable runs from one light position to the next, emerging as a loop through each ceiling hole **6**. Cut the cable at each light position and connect the cores to the transformer terminals **7**. Then plug the light fitting directly into the output terminals. Insert the transformer into the ceiling void through the ceiling hole **8**, and clip the light fitting into place. Repeat for the other fittings, then restore the power supply and test the lights.

central heating problems

Like most householders, you probably take your central heating system very much for granted. You assume that everything is fine, as long as it comes on when it is supposed to and the cylinder is full of hot water when you want a bath. But problems and faults can develop as time goes by. Since calling out a plumber can be expensive (especially at 10 o'clock on a Sunday night), it pays to learn how to tackle the most common minor faults yourself. Here are some of the basics jobs you may need to undertake at some time or other.

MINOR REPAIRS AND LEAKS

Most central heating systems work by pumping hot water around a series of metal radiators. From time to time you may notice that one or more radiators are becoming cool at the top. This is caused by one of two faults. The system may be losing water as a result of evaporation from the feed-and-expansion tank in the loft, or because of a pinhole leak somewhere in the pipework (probably below the ground floor, where such a leak may go unnoticed). Air is drawn into the system and collects in the radiators, causing cool spots. Alternatively, corrosion somewhere in the system may be producing hydrogen gas, which collects in the same way.

The cure is to 'bleed' the affected radiator(s). All you need is a radiator bleed key, which you can buy from DIY stores and plumber's merchants. On some modern radiators, the air vent can be opened with a screwdriver.

Locate the air vent in the top corner of the radiator, then insert the bleed key or screwdriver tip and turn it to open the vent. You will hear air or gas hissing out. Keep the vent open until water (which will probably be very dirty) starts to emerge. Catch it with some kitchen roll or an old towel before it drips down the edge of the radiator **1**. Close the air vent, using the bleed key or screwdriver. Repeat for the other affected radiators if necessary.

After bleeding the radiators, check that the feed-and-expansion tank is at least one-third full of water. It should be topped up via the ball valve in the tank, but if filling is not needed regularly, this valve may have jammed shut through lack of use. Depress the float arm so that the tank fills up to the required level, and check to see that it shuts off again.

NOISES IN THE PIPEWORK

The pipework in a heating system expands as it heats up and contracts as it cools down. This can cause creaking noises due to pipes moving against timber joists and other surfaces, and is nothing to worry about. The problem can be alleviated by adjusting the positions of pipe clips, and by providing a pad of insulation between pipes and adjacent surfaces.

The sound of rushing water in the pipes when the heating comes on suggests that there is air in the system. Bleed this off at a radiator, and check that there is enough water in the feed-and-expansion tank (see above). Contact a heating engineer for advice if the problem persists.

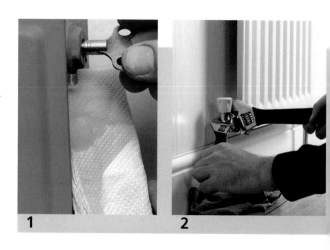

1 2

A humming sound in the pipework may be caused by pump vibration, or by too high a pump speed. Anti-vibration brackets fitted to the pipework at either side of the pump may help, as will reducing the pump speed to a lower setting.

Noises in the boiler suggest a build-up of scale in the system. The simplest cure is to add a chemical cleaner and de-scaling solution to the system at the feed-and-expansion tank. Follow the manufacturer's instructions.

MINOR REPAIRS AND LEAKS

A leak from the central heating is not a very common occurrence, but if it happens you need to know what to do to minimise the mess and disruption it can cause. The leak may occur at a fitting (commonly at a radiator connection), at a radiator, or somewhere on the system pipework. Because the contents of the system are often heavily contaminated by brown or black sludge, it is essential to contain the leak and fix it promptly.

CURING A LEAKING FITTING

Valves connect each end of a radiator to the system pipework. If one leaks, use two adjustable spanners to tighten the connecting nuts and see if that cures the leak. Grip the valve body with one spanner to prevent it from twisting and fracturing the pipe below. Use the other spanner to tighten the cap-nut connecting the valve to the radiator **2**. Move the spanner upwards at the left-hand valve and downwards at the right-hand one. Grip the

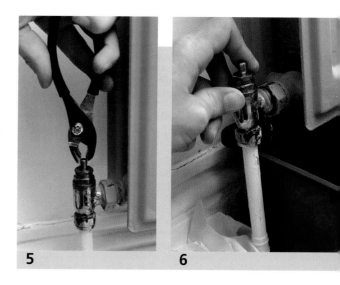

5   6

valve body with one spanner and use the other to tighten the cap-nut connecting the valve to the pipe below **3**. Move the spanner to the right at either valve.

DEALING WITH A RADIATOR LEAK

Leaks usually develop along the bottom or side seams of old panel radiators, and are caused by internal corrosion. If a leak occurs, prompt action is essential to minimise damage to floor coverings. Put polythene sheeting or bags under the leak, and add kitchen paper or an old towel to absorb it. Close down the handwheel valve, or thermostat, at one end of the radiator **4**. Remove the cover from the other valve and use pliers or a small spanner to close it **5**.

Unscrew the cap-nut at one end of the radiator. Hold the valve with another spanner to stop it from turning and fracturing the pipe below it. Place a shallow container underneath the valve and open the air vent at the top of the radiator with a bleed key (see opposite). Stop the flow to empty the container, if necessary, by tightening the cap-nut **6**. When no more water flows out, undo the cap-nut connecting the other valve to the radiator. Lift the radiator off its brackets (get help if it is a long radiator) and drain off any remaining water. Plug the radiator outlets with rolled-up kitchen paper and carry the radiator outside. The rest of the heating system will continue to operate as normal until you are ready to replace this radiator with a new one (see page 77).

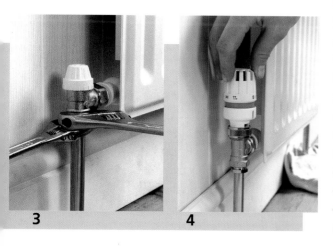

3   4

home security & safety

Security is a major concern for householders everywhere, while personal safety issues are paramount, especially when it comes to protection against the risks of fire. You can take simple steps to safeguard your home against a break-in and, in the event of an undetected fire, save those inside from the potentially fatal effects of smoke inhalation.

SECURING YOUR HOME

The best way to ensure that your home will deter burglars without forcing you to live in a prison is to evaluate its weak spots and take the necessary steps to provide an adequate level of security. Contact the Crime Prevention Officer attached to your local police force for advice on all aspects of home security. Also ask your household insurance company to find out what their security requirements are, and whether they will offer a discount to insure a well-secured house. The following security checklist will help you to do this effectively.

● Make sure your front door is secure by adding a mortise lock to supplement the cylinder rim lock that is usually fitted as standard. The lock should be made to British Standard BS3621 (see page 30).

1

2

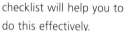

3

● Add a security chain or bar to prevent forced entry when you open the door to callers **1**.
● Fit a door viewer on a solid door so you can identify callers **2**. Fitting a door viewer is really easy. All it needs is a hole of the right size, then you screw together the two parts of the viewer through the hole. Take time drilling the hole to make sure it is absolutely square to the door.
👍 **TOP TIP When drilling a hole you can normally see if the drill is pointing to the left or the right, but it is less easy to see if it's going up or down. Ask someone to stand outside, around 3m (10ft) away, and they will be able to tell you instantly.**
● Fit hinge bolts to the hinged edge of the door to protect it from being forced.
● Side or back doors usually have a mortise sashlock fitted as standard. Upgrade yours to a BS3621 model, and add surface-mounted bolts at top and bottom for night-time security. Fit hinge bolts, too, if the door opens outwards.
● Modern patio doors usually have secure multi-point locks. Add surface-mounted door bolts to old-style doors at top and bottom to prevent them from being lifted off their tracks.
● Fit surface-mounted locks to all downstairs windows **3**, and to any upstairs ones that can be reached with or without a ladder. Consider fitting laminated glass to vulnerable windows and door panes.
● Fit locking bolts to a side gate to prevent easy access to the rear of the house. Fit padlocks and steel clasps to outbuildings to prevent theft of tools and equipment that could be used to aid a burglary. Padlock ladders stored outdoors to sturdy wall brackets.

4

● Consider a burglar alarm system, but remember that a ringing alarm is more likely to trigger local annoyance than any useful neighbourly response. A monitored alarm is worth considering if you live in a remote location. Otherwise, a dummy alarm box or dummy camera **4** may prove a much less expensive deterrent.

FIRE SAFETY

It is every householder's responsibility to ensure that family members can escape in the event of a fire. This means planning two escape routes. One should be via the stairs, with a set of front door keys kept somewhere accessible so the door can be unlocked quickly in an emergency. The other is for use if the stairs are impassable, and should be via an upstairs window – ideally on to a flat roof, or over a grassed or planted area. Keys for any window locks should be kept close to the designated window. Fitting automatic door closers **5** will confine a fire to one room.

Your boiler should have a ventilator of the right size (as recommended by the manufacturer) fitted to an outside wall, as a boiler starved of air will create carbon monoxide gas – an invisible but lethal gas that has no smell. You can install a detector next to the boiler for this type of gas **6**.

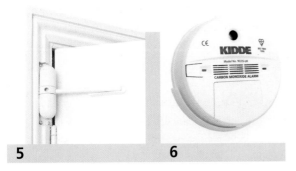

5 **6**

make sure everyone in the family knows what to do in the event of a fire and where the keys are kept

HOME SAFETY

The two most important things you can do to protect your home and its occupants from the dangers of fire are to install smoke detectors and to plan an escape route to be used in the event of a fire.

● Battery-powered smoke detectors **A** are inexpensive to buy and can be installed in minutes. Make sure that any detector you buy is made to British Standard BS5446. Fit one on each floor of the house, on the hall and landing ceilings away from room corners. Do not install one in a kitchen,

A

where cooking fumes can trigger regular false alarms. The exception is if you regularly use a washing machine, tumble drier or dishwasher after going to bed; a smoke detector will alert you in the unlikely event of a machine malfunction. Test the battery at least once a month, and replace the battery once a year – on a notable date,

B

such as your birthday. Never remove the battery to use it in another appliance.

● For additional safety, buy a fire blanket **B** made to British Standard BS EN1869 and a powder-type fire extinguisher made to BS EN3 **C**. The former will douse chip-pan fires, and the latter will cope with most other small domestic fires. Keep them both in the kitchen, where they are most likely to be needed.

C

front doors

You can improve the security of your house considerably by adding new locks and other security devices to your front door – and adding a letterbox and a doorknocker are both worthwhile improvements, otherwise how will you know when the postman's delivering you a mysterious parcel or letter?

FITTING A NEW DOOR LOCK AND LETTERBOX

If you only have a simple Yale lock on the front door (technically known as a 'nightlatch'), it is easy to replace it with a secure door lock. What you need is a surface-mounted replacement 'rim' lock and you should choose the type that is designed to replace an existing nightlatch. Check its rating – for full security, you want a lock made to the British Standard (BS3621).

Unscrew the old lock from the door **1**. Normally, you unscrew the lock body first, undo the screws in the plate below and take out the cylinder lock from the other side **2**. Also remove the striking plate from the door frame.

Clean and sand down the paintwork just around the lock and fill any scratches (you can repaint later if necessary). If you have bought the type of lock designed to replace a nightlatch, this should be straightforward, though a bit of fine chiselling may be necessary to fit the end of the lock snugly into the door. Full instructions are provided with the lock, but you already have the most

difficult part – the large hole in the door. You will need a hacksaw to cut the flat connecting bar of the lock to match the thickness of the door **3**. Don't cut it too short or the lock won't work.

Fit the new striking plate to the frame. With the lock in place on the door, close the door so you can mark the position of the lock on the frame **4**. Then hold the new striking plate against the frame in line with your marks **5**, so you can work out whether you need to chisel away any wood in order to fit it.

👍 **TOP TIP The screws provided with locks are often on the short side. For added security, buy longer ones of the same gauge and use these instead.**

Where the new lock is smaller than the old one, there may be some gaps left **6**. These can be filled with plastic wood, or, if you have the time, with small bits of wood glued into place, which you can then chisel down to give a smooth finish.

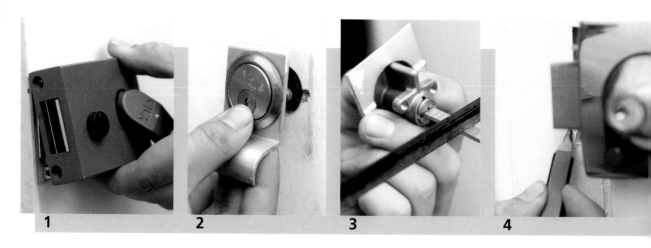

1   2   3   4

👍 **TOP TIP** If an existing lock is not working properly, you can normally replace just the cylinder. Take the old cylinder to the shop with you to make sure you get exactly the right size.

OTHER DOOR FURNITURE

Door knobs and knockers are easy to fit, especially with a helper. Just mark the position on the door, drill holes for the securing screws and fit at the back.

A letterbox is slightly more complicated. Using the new letterbox as a guide **7**, start by marking out the size of hole needed on the outside of the door **8**. Drill a 10mm (⅜in) hole in each corner of the marked outline **9**, large enough to take the blade of a padsaw or a jigsaw. At the same time, drill the two extra holes needed to take the securing bolts of the letter box. Cut the four sides of the rectangle. A jigsaw makes the job a lot easier, but needs great care in use **10**. Fit and tighten the securing bolts at the back of the letter box and fit it in place **11**.

KEEPING THE WEATHER OUT

Not all doors have a weatherboard – a curved moulding on the outside bottom of the door to shed rain. Fitting one is fairly simple – just cut the board to length (if necessary) and drill three screw holes through it. Fix the weatherboard to the door using rustproof screws.

interior doors

Lots of things can go wrong with doors – they can rattle, they can bind (not shut properly), they can scrape on the floor and they can squeak. Fortunately, all of these things can be solved fairly simply.

MINOR REPAIRS

A door normally rattles because it has shrunk or warped slightly so that the latch is no longer making correct contact with the keeper plate in the frame. You can solve this by moving the keeper a little closer to the frame. First measure the gap between the closed door and the frame, then unscrew the old keeper **1** and drill out the screw holes using a 6mm (¼in) dowelling bit **2**. Glue dowels into the holes with a little bit protruding **3** and allow the glue to dry. Chisel off the end **4**, then chisel out the recess for the keeper at the back so that it fits further into the door frame **5**. Mark new screw holes and use a bradawl to start them off. Re-fit the keeper and try the door – if you have moved the keeper too far, use a metal file to increase the size of the slot, don't try to move it again.

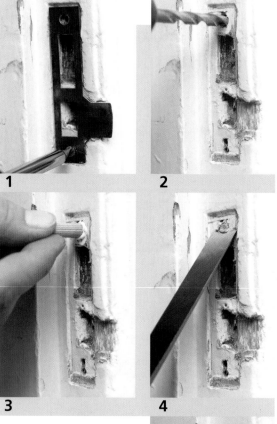

CURING A BINDING DOOR

When a door doesn't shut properly, it could be due to one of four things: loose hinge screws, a hinge that is not sufficiently recessed, a swollen door or worn hinges.

To rectify a loose hinge, first try tightening the screws in both the door and the frame side of the hinge. If the screws won't tighten, replace them with longer ones of the same gauge

Hinges should be flush (level) with the door frame and with the door. If the recesses are not set deeply enough and binding, remove the door, deepen the recesses with a chisel, and re-hang the door. If the recesses are too deep, pack them out with slivers of cardboard.

👍 **TOP TIP** You can use a coin to measure a small gap between a door and its frame:
1p = 1.5mm   2p = 2mm
£2 = 2.5mm   £1 = 3mm

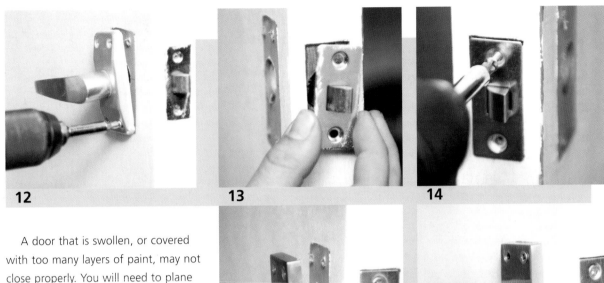

12   13   14

15   16

A door that is swollen, or covered with too many layers of paint, may not close properly. You will need to plane material off the closing edge of the door – something that is much easier to do with the door removed. Sometimes, you only need to plane the leading edge of the door (the one that meets the frame first): check the closing of the door against the frame before removing it. Plane from the door ends towards the middle.

SQUEAKING

Have you thought of oiling the door hinges? Try it – you'll be amazed. Place some kitchen paper on the floor first to catch any drips.

REPLACING DOOR LOCKS

Interior door locks are generally easy to replace, as they are either simple mortise latches operated by a handle or, in older houses, larger two-bolt mortice locks with both a handle and a key-operated lock.

You can usually remove the handle by unscrewing the plate holding it on **12** or for a simple knob, remove the tiny screw. Then you can withdraw the square bar which passes through the old lock. Unscrew the latch from the door and remove it **13** (lever it out with a screwdriver if necessary). Take the lock to the shop to make sure that you get an exact replacement. Screw in the new latch **14**.

You can fit any type of handle to an interior door **15** – if you are fitting a new square bar, this may need cutting down (with a hacksaw, see page 30) in order to suit the thickness of door. Screw on the new handle **16**.

FIXING A SCRAPING DOOR

If the door is scraping on the floor, it may simply be that the top hinge screws need tightening. If the door has swollen, you may be able to reduce the height a bit by laying some sandpaper on the floor and passing the door over it a few times. But if you have fitted new floorcoverings, you may have to take the door off and plane or cut it down using a circular or panel saw.

👍 **TOP TIP Most carpet fitters carry a special saw, which they use for cutting the bottoms off doors. This can be carried out without removing the doors. For convenience, you might find it well worth paying for this to be done.**

decorative mouldings

Timber and plaster mouldings play a functional as well as an aesthetic role – they hide the joints between different building materials – so it is important to maintain or restore them. Copies of period mouldings are readily available and even a very old and intricate moulding can be reproduced by specialised timber millers and fibrous plaster specialists.

WOODEN MOULDINGS

ARCHITRAVES

Architraves are mainly found around door openings. The profiles can be fairly plain in modern houses or extremely ornate in older properties. Splits and holes in simple architrave are easy to repair with wood filler, but you may have to search, and improvise, to match the original shape in an ornate architrave.

Door architraves are secured to the hidden frame underneath in three pieces – the two sides and the top – by oval nails. To remove the architrave, run a trimming knife along both edges to break the paint film and lever the moulding away from the wall, using an old chisel resting on a wooden block.

The two top corners of door architrave need to be mitred – that is, cut at 45 degrees so they form a joint. This is easily done with a mitre saw, but a humble mitre block, in which you rest your tenon saw, will do the job equally well **1**. Double-check that you are cutting the angle the correct way round – it is easy to get it wrong.

Cut the two side pieces to the same length, with the mitres at the top corners, and secure them with oval nails, using a spirit level to make sure they are perfectly aligned **2**. Then hold the top piece in place and mark out the ends of the two mitre cuts. Cut these mitres and fit the top piece in the same way.

👍 **TOP TIP To prevent the mitres from opening up, nail down through the top section of architrave into the two sides.**

1

2

3

4   **5**

with ornate mouldings, you may have to build up a replacement using two, or three, different sections

SKIRTING BOARDS

Skirtings fit along the bottom of walls to hide the gap between wall and floor and to protect the wall plaster. Builders usually fit skirtings with cut nails (square-section nails, similar to those used to hold down floorboards), but it is easier to replace them with screws into wallplugs (or, for partition walls, into the vertical studs). As with architraves, skirtings can be plain or ornate – and if you are replacing a section, it is worth making the effort to find an exact replacement.

To remove skirting, the best tool is a wrecking bar. Start in the middle of a length rather than at the end, and be prepared to repair any damage and marking to the wall (see pages 37–39) before you fit the new skirting. To avoid damaging and marking the wall, insert a flat piece of wood behind the bar.

There are two ways to deal with corners when fitting skirting – mitres (see opposite) and scribing. Mitring

(cutting the ends of the skirting to 45 degrees) is always used at external corners. Scribing (cutting the end of one board to match the profile of the board it meets) is used for internal corners. Board ends can also be mitred where two lengths of skirting join along a wall, so that one mitre fits behind the other – this is called scarfing.

The simplest way to cut a mitre in a skirting board is to use a mitre saw, with the blade set to 45 degrees. To cut a scribed end, rest a square piece of moulding at right angles to the back of the length to be cut and draw round the shape with a pencil **3**, before cutting the shape with a coping saw or a jigsaw **4**. You may need to make more than one cut if there is an intricate pattern.

Before screwing the skirting in place, drill holes for the screws and mark through these to fit wallplugs in solid walls. In hollow walls, line the screw holes up with the wall studs, which should be obvious when the skirting is removed. Fill over the screw heads before painting **5**.

PLASTER MOULDINGS

CORNICES

Cornices are fitted to cover the gap between wall and ceiling. With an ornate plaster cornice, you may want to dig out the encrusted paint to reveal the original profile; a small pointed stick and lots of water will do the job, but be patient – it will take time.

Adding a cornice is a simple job if you use one of the modern lightweight polystyrene mouldings (these are simply glued into place), but fitting traditional plaster mouldings requires more care. It is probably best to fit the cornice prior to decorating. You will need to cut the required mortices at internal and external corners (see Architraves, page 34) in addition to using adhesive, which needs to be applied on the two sides of the curve **1**, you will normally have to drill holes in the plaster moulding to fit screws into the wall after pushing it into place **2**. You need to clean off the excess adhesive and make good any gaps between the cornice and the wall with plaster filler.

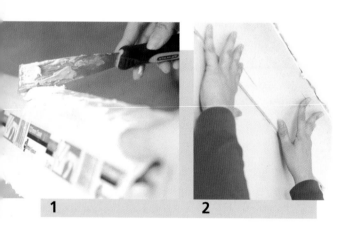

1   2

DADO RAILS

Dado rails are traditionally positioned at waist height around a room to protect the wall from damage caused by chair backs. Adding a dado rail can be easy if you use one of the timber mouldings that are fitted by a clever click-on system, otherwise you will have to screw sections of timber moulding on to a completely flat wall. Any dips can be filled beforehand and sanded for a smooth surface.

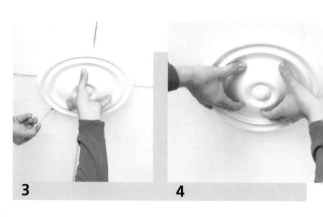

3   4

CEILING ROSES

These come in choice of polystyrene or plaster. Polystyrene ceiling centres are easy to fit, requiring only adhesive. Plaster ceiling roses are relatively heavy, so need to be held up with screws driven up into the ceiling joists, as well as adhesive; otherwise the whole lot might come crashing down! You will need to establish the position of these joists with a joist detector before fixing the ceiling rose.

Find the centre of the ceiling by using two lines of string stretched diagonally from opposite corners of the ceiling. Mark the position of the ceiling rose on the ceiling by drawing round it with a pencil, centred on where the strings intersect **3**.

Seal the ceiling and the back of the rose with a coat of dilute PVA adhesive. Apply some plaster or tile adhesive to the back of the rose, then press firmly into place **4**. Wipe off any excess glue. If you have a central ceiling light (see pages 20–21), make a hole in the ceiling rose and pull the lighting flex through before fixing the rose **5**. Paint the ceiling rose to finish.

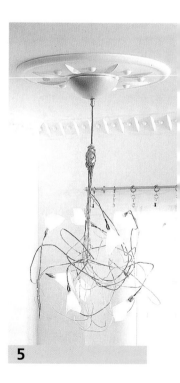

5

preparing for decorating

I can hear my dad saying to me time and again, all those years ago, 'The finish is only as good as the prep work that goes into it!' How right he was! You can expect to spend two days preparing and half an hour painting, rather than the other way round. Above all, you should repair and seal all old and damaged plaster before decorating.

PLASTER

A cracked, unstable or damp-damaged plaster surface will spoil any paint that is applied to it, so be sure to remedy any problems before you start decorating. If you paint over new plaster that has not dried out properly, dusty old plaster, existing flaking paintwork, a greasy surface – usually in a kitchen – or a damp wall, the new paintwork will start to flake in a relatively short time.

NEW PLASTER

New plaster is porous so it must be sealed (primed) before it can be painted, whether you intend to paint the plaster directly or to cover it with lining paper first. As it must be completely dry before this can be done, allow at least 4 weeks after plastering before you start work.

Use either diluted PVA adhesive (5 parts water to 1 part PVA) or diluted emulsion paint (1 part water to 8 parts emulsion) to prime the wall. Apply liberally **1**.

OLD PLASTER AND PAINTWORK

Old, bare plaster often has a dusty coating that comes off on the hand. Such walls need to be coated with a stabilizing primer to prevent fresh paint from flaking off **2**; water-diluted PVA adhesive (see above) is ideal. If the surface is not dusty, you can seal the plaster with diluted emulsion paint.

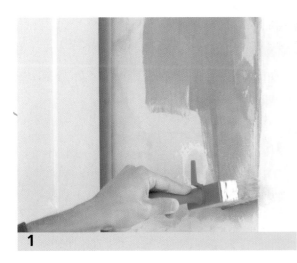

1

2

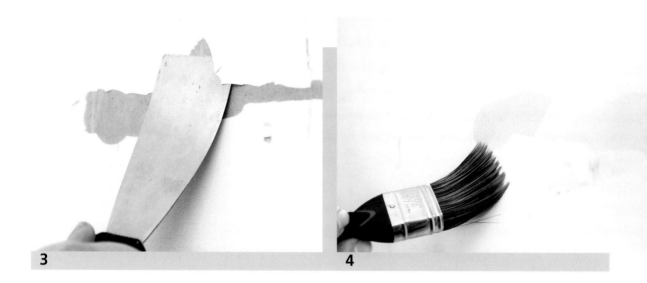

3

4

Old paintwork that is flaking needs to be scraped back with a paint scraper tool until only sound paintwork remains **3**. There is no short-cut here, just hard graft! When it is in a good state, coat the wall with stabilizing primer before decorating **4**. If the wall was painted previously and the covering is sound, just wash it all over with diluted sugar soap, then rinse with clean water. You can then paint it directly with emulsion.

DEALING WITH DAMP

If you just paint over a damp area the new paint will flake off in weeks, so where damp is suspected you must find the cause and remedy it before you do anything else. Damp plaster is normally caused by leaking or faulty rainwater goods (gutters or down pipes), or penetrating or rising damp caused by the external ground level bridging the damp-proof course. Lowering all external ground levels to 100–150mm (4–6in) below the damp-proof course, and repairing or replacing leaking or damaged rainwater goods should solve most damp problems. Penetrating damp can be caused by a crack or a porous wall – fill cracks and apply silicone water repellent or paint with masonry paint.

Even after a damp problem has been rectified, a dried stain is often left behind. This must be sealed, otherwise the stain will reappear through the new paint after it has dried. Stabilizing solution and aluminium primer sealers are the best products for covering an old damp stain if a wide area is affected. However, if only a small patch is stained, then it is much more economical to use an aerosol spray sold as stain-block under various brand names **5**. Alternatively, block out the stain with an oil based paint and leave it to dry before applying two coats of emulsion.

👍 **TOP TIP Beware damp-proofing experts! Most companies suggest taking off and replacing the plaster, rather than fixing the cause of the damp plaster. A specialist surveyor of damp problems stated that in 98% of cases, the repair work was unnecessary and didn't solve the real problem.**

5

FILLING CRACKS

The amount of preparation needed beyond priming and stabilizing, depends on the overall condition of the wall. If you are going to paint with emulsion, even hairline cracks must be filled, otherwise they will be visible after you have decorated. Use ordinary cellulose filler, sold ready-mixed or in powder form for mixing with water, for fine cracks. A broad-bladed filling knife or caulking blade will get the job done quickly **6**. The alternative is to cover the entire wall with lining paper (see page 44) or a wallcovering that is specially manufactured to be painted over.

You can fill larger cracks and holes with cellulose filler, too. First, undercut the crack with the edge of a filling knife to widen the gap below the surface and so give the filler a good anchor. Use an old brush to clean away the dust, then dampen the crack or hole with water to lengthen the filler's drying time **7**; this reduces the likelihood of the filler shrinking. Apply the filler with a filling knife, dragging it across the crack first of all **8**, then drawing it down the crack to smooth it off. If you can achieve a smooth finish with a filling knife, all well and good, if not, leave the filler slightly proud, then smooth it off when it is dry, using sandpaper **9**.

For large holes, you can use a deep-crack filler, though plaster filler is more economical. Apply it with a trowel in layers no deeper than 12mm (½in), allowing each layer to set before applying the next **10**. Where movement is likely, such as around a door architrave or skirting boards, use a flexible filler or sealant supplied in a cartridge **11**. This will keep the crack closed despite any movement. Cracks running along the top of a wall where it meets the ceiling are caused by normal house movement; they will continue to re-open if filled, so they are best concealed behind a coving.

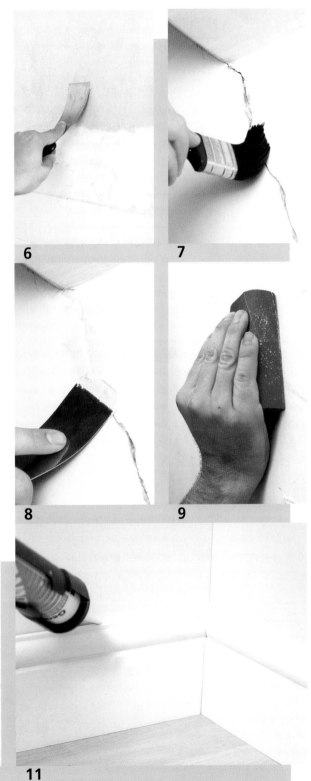

6

7

8

9

10

11

decorating your home

Should I be bold and choose strong, contemporary colours to make a statement, or is it safer to go for an understated look with subtle pastel shades? The answer is, please yourself! There is now an amazing array of paint products to choose from. Although seemingly bewildering at first, this vast choice enables you to produce top-quality work more easily and to select not only the precise shade, but also the texture and thickness of paint you require.

PAINT TYPES

Almost all paints used in the home are either water- or solvent-based. Modern water-based paints are easier to use and more environmentally friendly than traditional solvent-based paints, based on white spirit, which are often the choice of professional decorators.

Primer A watery product used to seal a bare surface and form a base for other paint coats, to prevent them sinking into the surface. For bare wood, plaster or metal. Match a specific product to the surface – for example, use plaster primer for new plaster. All-purpose primers are available but are not generally considered as good as the specific types.

Undercoat Gives a hard-wearing matt finish and provides an excellent base for the application of top coat(s). It has good covering properties and can be used on any primed surface. Where it is painted over old gloss, apply one or two coats as necessary to completely obliterate the old colour.

Primer undercoat A combined product of primer and undercoat used on bare wood, providing a sound base for top coat(s). It's easy and quick to use, though some people prefer separate primer and undercoat.

Matt emulsion Water-based paint for giving a flat finish. For use on bare plaster, though it is not hard-wearing. A diluted first coat is often used before the full-strength finishing coat(s).

Vinyl, silk, satin and eggshell emulsion Used on primed or previously painted surfaces, or over lining paper or textured wallcoverings. Water-based, hard-wearing and easy to clean. A paint described as, for example, 'silk', can produce a slightly different texture from brand to brand.

Gloss A shiny, hard-wearing top-quality paint for use on undercoated surfaces, normally wood or metal. Oil-based and very easy to clean. It has to be applied carefully to get quality results.

Textured paint Used on plaster, especially that which is rough and needs to be covered. It can be finished in a variety of patterns from stippled to swirls. It gives a surface texture to flat walls but takes time to apply. It is difficult to clean, and hard to remove later on.

Floor paint Although it can be used on wood (see page 83), this is mainly intended for concrete, brick and stone. A hard-wearing, easy to clean product that combats a dusty surface and brightens the floors of garages, utility rooms etc.

Eggshell A matt, oil-based top coat that is tough and specially good for covering old woodwork because it doesn't reflect imperfections, like gloss.

There is now a range of speciality paints which can be used, for example, on melamine surfaces, to combat condensation or to hide the effects of damp. These paints are always sold with specific names stating the precise purpose of the product, making selection easy.

SHEEN LEVELS

Modern top coat paints come in different levels of sheen, or gloss; the level of sheen determines whether the paint will absorb or reflect light. Choose a sheen according to the room being decorated and how much wear and tear it has to withstand.

Matt A flat finish which masks flaws in a surface. It is susceptible to scuff marks, however, though there is now a small choice of wipeable matt emulsions.

Silk or satin vinyl emulsion More or less identical, these are more wipeable than a matt finish and so are a popular choice for hard-working areas such as kitchens, bathrooms, children's rooms and hallways. (This kind of paint is sometimes referred to as eggshell by some manufacturers).

Satinwood or semi-gloss Most commonly used on woodwork, this finish falls somewhere in between the above levels of sheen.

Gloss Makes a surface shiny and smooth. It is normally used only on woodwork as it highlights imperfections and would therefore rarely be used on walls. It doesn't attract dirt and can be readily wiped down.

HOW MUCH PAINT DO YOU NEED?

Knowing how much paint is required for a room is a matter of determining the overall area of the walls, then making a deduction for the doors, large picture windows and patio doors. Any guide is an approximation, as some surfaces are more porous than others, so the suggested figures should be used in conjunction with the manufacturer's advice. Multiply the figure by the number of coats likely to be needed.

There are several other variables involved which can affect how much paint you need for a job, the type of paint and the old paint colour being the main factors. For example, if you are painting over old gloss, it may take a couple of coats to obliterate the old colour completely – as you must do before using gloss top coat. A darker emulsion might take three coats to cover it completely, whereas when a dark colour is going over a pale one, it will usually need only two coats.

PAINT COVERAGE PER LITRE

TYPE OF PAINT	SQ. M	(SQ. FT)
all-purpose primer	9–11	(100–120)
plaster primer	5–9	(55–100)
metal primer	11–13	(120–140)
primer undercoat	15–16	(160–170)
undercoat	15–16	(160–170)
matt emulsion	14–16	(150–170)
silk and satin emulsion	15–16	(160–170)
gloss	15–17	(160–180)

use the chart as a guide only – the porosity of the surface and the density of the colour beneath may affect the paint coverage

PLAYING WITH COLOUR

● Bring down a high ceiling by painting it in a bold or advancing colour. Continue this colour down to a cornice or picture rail if you want to lower it further. And if the floor covering is a similar colour to the ceiling, this will visually lower a tall room even more.

● Make a low ceiling seem less oppressive by painting it white or a pale receding shade **1**.

4

CALCULATING WALLPAPER QUANTITIES

ESTIMATING THE NUMBER OF ROLLS

WALL HEIGHT:	2.5m (8ft)	2.75m (9ft)	3m (10ft)
9m (30ft)	5	6	6
10.5m (34ft)	5	6	7
11.5m (38ft)	6	7	8
12.75m (42ft)	7	7	8
14m (46ft)	7	8	9
15m (50ft)	8	9	10
16.5m (54ft)	9	9	10
17.75m (58ft)	9	10	11
19m (62ft)	10	10	12
20m (66ft)	10	11	13
21.25m (70ft)	11	12	13
22.5m (74ft)	12	12	14
24m (78ft)	12	13	15

(DISTANCE AROUND ROOM (INCLUDING DOORS AND WINDOWS))

● Allow extra wallpaper for wastage or pattern matching
● Four lengths of paper can usually be cut per roll, but if the pattern is very large, you may only get three, or possibly two, lengths out of a roll to allow for pattern matching.

● Broaden a narrow hallway by painting the end walls in a dark or warm colour and the side walls in a pale, receding shade. The same technique will also make a rectangular room look longer **2**.

● To turn a fireplace or large piece of furniture into a focal point, paint the wall behind it in a stronger or more vibrant colour than the rest of the room **3**.

● The light-reflecting sheen of silk vinyl or satin emulsion makes the most of natural light and will help a low-ceilinged room look brighter **4**.

● Features such as radiators and built-in cupboards will be less conspicuous if they are painted the same colour as the surrounding walls. In small rooms, the doors can also be painted to merge with their surroundings.

wallpapering

The first time I used wallpaper was as a young schoolboy, and that was to cover all my school books. Unfortunately for me, the only wallpaper we had was what remained after papering my granny's bedroom – a design with huge pink roses on a cream and pink background. Boy, did I get some stick for that! Selecting wallpaper has remained a thorny subject ever since!

EQUIPMENT AND PREPARATION

Wallpapering isn't as difficult as it looks once you are equipped with the necessary tools (see page 12). In addition to a paste table, brushes and some paste, you will also need shears, a spirit level, plumb line, scraping tools and sandpaper. Stairwells are the most problematic area and they are covered separately (see page 49).

CALCULATING THE NUMBER OF ROLLS

To calculate how many rolls you need to buy, get hold of a wallpaper-calculating chart, readily available from most DIY stores or see page 43. Measure the height of the walls from skirting board to the ceiling, coving, picture or dado rail (depending how far up you intend to cover) and the perimeter of the room. (Don't deduct anything for the areas covered by doors or windows, unless there is a large picture window or patio door.) On the chart, find the measurement nearest to the perimeter of your room in the left-hand column then read across to find the height of the room in the right-hand column. There you will find the number of rolls required for a plain wallpaper.

If the wallpaper has a pattern you may need to take this into account. A large pattern repeat requires more paper than a random or non-matching design, which doesn't need to be pattern matched. The best bet is to buy an extra roll on a sale-or-return

basis, so that if you don't need to open it, you will get your money back. Check when buying that the batch number printed on the label of each roll is the same **1**. Even then, a slight difference in shading is possible, so you need to unroll all the paper at home and examine the colours in a good light. If any of the rolls are of a slightly different shade, don't hang them on the same wall, where the difference might be noticeable.

PREPARING THE WALLS

Before you hang the wallpaper, prepare the walls in the same way as for painting (see pages 37–39). However, where the old plaster is sound but badly crazed, or has been repaired in places over the years, it is best to hang lining paper first **2**, as this will prevent defects showing through the wallpaper. Lining paper is usually hung horizontally **3**, to prevent the joints coinciding with the wallpaper.

Any existing wallcovering must be stripped off completely. Some papers can be stripped off in lengths

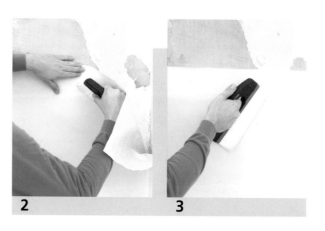

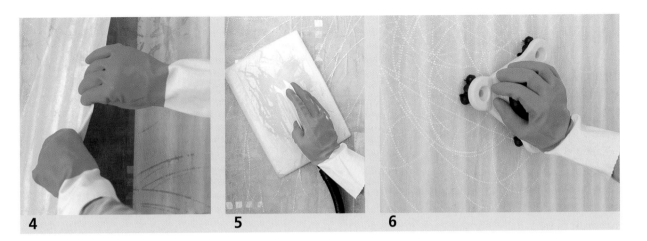

4   5   6

simply by loosening the bottom edge and pulling upwards **4**. This leaves a thin backing paper on the wall which should be wetted then scraped off. Other wallcoverings may need to be soaked with water before scraping them off. Adding a little wallpaper paste or washing up liquid to the water helps the soaking process, making the stripping easier afterwards. Some vinyls and washable wallcoverings will need to be scored first, to allow water to penetrate the old paste.

If you are faced with a really stubborn wallpaper, or more than one layer, you can save time and effort by hiring or buying a wallpaper steam stripper **5**. This produces steam through a square plate that loosens the paper when it is held against the wall. It's a great labour-saving device and quite inexpensive to buy these days. Recently some clever cookie invented a handy little tool called an orbital scorer, which you simply run over the

paper in a circular motion **6**, creating little pin holes that allow the moisture from the steamer to penetrate behind the surface. After doing this, use both a broad-bladed and narrow-bladed scraping knife to carefully remove the old paper without damaging the plaster behind **7**.

When all the paper has been stripped off, rub the walls down with sandpaper to remove any little nibs of paper still clinging to them **8**.

Porous walls have to be 'sized' to ensure that the wallpaper adheres properly; sizing has the added bonus of making it easier to slide the paper into place when pattern matching across the lengths. Size can be bought purpose-made (a powder that is mixed with water) or you can simply dilute ordinary wallpaper paste, according to the manufacturer's instructions. Brush size on to the wall **9** and leave it to dry for a short while before hanging the wallpaper.

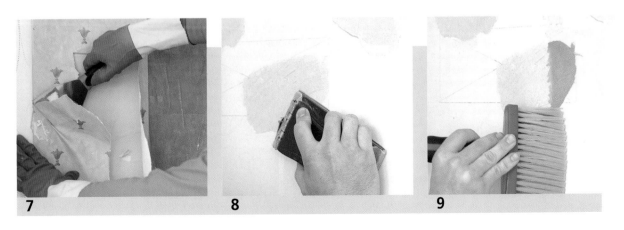

7   8   9

HANGING WALLPAPER

All the wall preparation is complete, the paintwork looks superb, now for the wallpapering! You will undoubtedly have more than enough paper (just in case you make the occasional cock up!), all the necessary tools, and of course will be dressed in your decorating overalls.

Normally, you start papering on the window wall, then work back into the room. This way, should any adjoining lengths be inadvertently overlapped (they are not supposed to be), a shadow could not be cast on the overlap and highlight the error. The exception to this rule is where the wallpaper features a large motif. In this case, for a balanced appearance, the motif needs to be centralized on the main focal point. For example, if there is a chimney breast in the room, the first length would be hung right in the middle of it.

Obviously, wallpaper must be hung vertically. To establish a vertical guideline, you can suspend a plumb line from the ceiling at your proposed starting point **1** and, when it stops swinging, use a straight-edge and pencil to mark its position on the wall **2**. The alternative is to use a 1m (3ft) spirit level. Whenever you take the paper round a corner, mark a vertical guideline for the first strip on the new wall **3**.

Measure each length and cut to size with wallpaper shears **4**, allowing an excess of about 50mm (2in) at the top and bottom, depending on the pattern repeat, for final trimming at the ceiling and skirting.

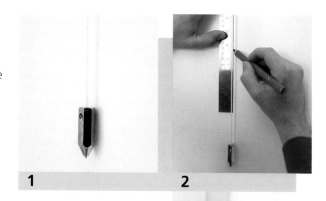

Mix up the wallpaper paste according to the manufacturer's instructions. It is best to work on a pasting table so you can lay out the whole length to paste.

Every bit of the backing must be covered with paste because, if you leave any dry spots, bubbling will result. First apply paste down the centre of the paper **5**, then brush out to the edges in a herringbone fashion **6**.

Vinyls and lightweight papers can be hung immediately after they are pasted, but other types should be left folded to soak for a few minutes before hanging. Fold the paper by taking the top and bottom edges to meet in the centre **7**.

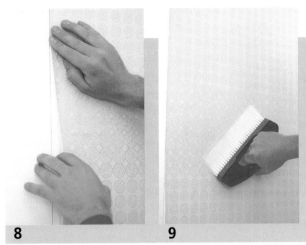

8

9

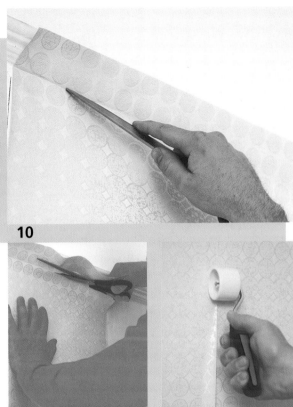

10

11

12

Without soaking, the paper will not adhere to the wall properly and bubbles will form. In the absence of any specific instructions, allow medium-weight paper about five minutes and heavyweights about ten minutes. Try to keep the soaking times for each length uniform or the wet paper may stretch irregularly when being brushed on the wall and cause problems in pattern matching.

When you are ready to hang the first length of paper, unfold the top half and align the edge with the vertical guideline **8**. Using a clean, dry wallpaper brush, brush down the centre of the paper, then work outwards to both edges to ensure there is no trapped air **9**. Release the bottom half of the paper and brush this out in the same way. At the top of the wall, run the back of the shears along the ceiling-to-wall juncture to leave a crease line **10**. Pull back the top of the paper, cut along the

crease line **11**, and brush the paper back into place. Trim the bottom of the paper at the skirting in the same way.

Hang the next and subsequent lengths in the same way, ensuring that you match the pattern if applicable. Butt up the edges closely. When adjoining lengths have been on the wall for a few minutes, run a seam roller down the join to ensure the edges are well stuck **12**. Don't use a seam roller on embossed paper, however.

CUTTING WHEEL

A cutting wheel is a neat gadget that allows you to trim the top and bottom of a length of wallpaper in situ, in a single operation.

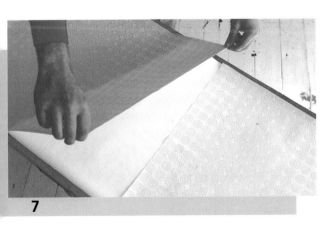

7

Never try to take a large amount of wallpaper round a corner. In an internal corner, measure the distance from the edge of the last length into the corner. Then take three measurements – at the top, middle and bottom – add 12mm (½in) to the largest measurement and cut a strip of this width from the next length of paper. (Three measurements are needed because few corners are exactly at right angles.) Hang the strip and brush the 12mm margin around the corner **1**. The remaining strip is then hung on the next wall and its edge brushed into the corner to overlap the 12mm margin **2**.

At external corners, take 50mm (2in) of paper on to the next wall. Hang the matching strip to overlap the 50mm margin. Then, using a straight-edge and sharp knife, cut down the middle of the overlap **3**, peel back the paper and carefully remove the two excess overlapping strips **4**. Brush the paper back into place and the edges of the two strips will butt up neatly **5**.

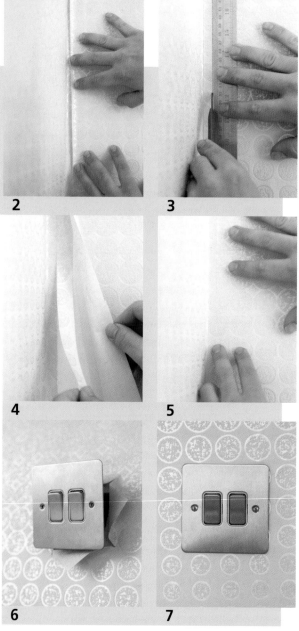

Where you meet a light switch, turn off the electricity supply to the switch and release the screws holding the faceplate in place, then pull the plate forward. Hang the paper down to the switch, then push the shears through the centre of the switchplate area and make a diagonal cut out to each corner **6**. Using small scissors, cut the paper around the switch, leaving a margin of about 6mm (¼in) behind the faceplate **7**. Screw the faceplate back in place and restore the electricity supply.

DECORATING A STAIRWELL

Access is the main problem when decorating a stairwell, and it is essential that you create a safe working platform to enable you to reach the walls and ceiling comfortably. A platform can comprise a hired scaffold system **8**, or a combination of ladders, stepladders and strong scaffold boards. Because stairwells and staircases vary tremendously, the arrangement of ladders and boards must be governed by the individual situation, and it is likely that you will have to rearrange the apparatus to reach different parts of the stairwell as you work. Always make sure that everything is secure before you climb up.

Staircase walls will need to be prepared for painting or papering in the usual way (see pages 44–47). You may have to paint or paper some walls first, then allow them to dry before you can lean a ladder against them in order to decorate adjacent walls.

👍 **TOP TIP Protect a newly decorated wall from damage by padding the tops of the ladders or steps that will have to be rested against them 9.**

The other problem with papering a stairwell is that you will be handling some extremely long lengths of wallpaper. The way around this is to fold the paper into a 'concertina' arrangement comprising several folds when pasting **10**. Because of the weight of pasted paper, it is important not to let the whole length drop down the wall in one go, as this will stretch it and make pattern matching impossible. With thinner paper, releasing it freely can cause it to tear.

Before cutting the lengths, measure very carefully. Unlike a normal wall, you have to allow for the staircase 'string' (the board that runs up the wall side of the staircase) being considerably lower at one bottom edge of the paper than at the other. This will become noticeable when you trim the paper **11**.

8

To prevent wastage from mistakes in measuring, the safest bet is to hang one length then measure up for the next. With a pattern that has to be matched, considerably more wastage is involved with staircase walls, so allow for this when calculating the number of rolls (see page 43).

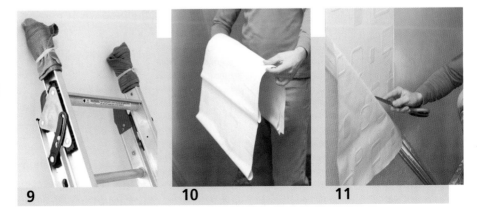

9   **10**   **11**

painting walls & doors

I really enjoy painting, as I find it very therapeutic, but it is vital to have the right equipment and techniques. For a successful paint finish, there is a method, a formula to guide you. Follow my tips and get in lots of practice and don't forget to clean-up afterwards!

BRUSHES AND ROLLERS

1

2

3

Having paintbrushes in a range of widths means you can always lay your hands on a paintbrush to suit the job

PAINTBRUSHES

Paintbrushes come in a range of sizes, and a standard kit of brushes 25, 50, 75 and 100 or 125mm (1, 2, 3, 4 or 5in) wide will cover all painting jobs around the home **1**. Use a narrow brush for painting fiddly areas, such as short sections, mouldings, or the glazing bars on windows. For whole walls, one of the larger sizes will cover a greater area per stroke. The sizes in between are for doors, skirtings, window sills and so on.

You might want to add a couple of special brushes to your collection **2**. A cutting-in brush has bristles cut at an angle for painting window frames without smudging the glass. (The alternative, unless you have a very steady hand, is to cover the glass with masking tape.) This type of brush comes in widths of 12, 18 and 25mm (½, ¾ and 1in). A radiator brush has a long handle for reaching down behind radiators, so they don't have to be taken off the wall. A paint kettle allows you to decant large tins of paint.

Most paintbrushes are made of natural animal bristle. Treated with care, these will last forever. They are the professional's choice – in fact I feel that, like men, they improve with age, giving the smoothest possible finish.

Brushes made with synthetic fibres are fine for water-based paint. The bristles of the most expensive synthetic brushes are made from polyester and nylon, and produce a better finish than cheaper types. Since they hold oil-based paint less well, synthetic fibres are only for rough work.

PAINT ROLLERS

Paint rollers are used mainly with emulsion paint for covering large areas like walls and ceilings, and they do the job faster than a brush **3**. Some people like to use small rollers to apply oil-based paint on flush doors and such like.

A paint roller consists of a handle and roller cage fitted with a sleeve, which applies the paint. Most sleeves are about 180mm (7in) long, though you can get wider ones which require more elbow work to drive them. Fibre sleeves may be natural or synthetic, but the type of fibre is less important than the length of pile, which is chosen according to the surface. Short pile sleeves are for smooth

4

surfaces, medium for slightly textured surfaces and long pile for uneven and deeply textured surfaces. Plastic foam sleeves are cheap but absorb a lot of paint and can cause splashes. You also need a roller tray into which you pour the paint. Load the roller by running it backwards and forwards in the paint **4**.

APPLYING THE PAINT

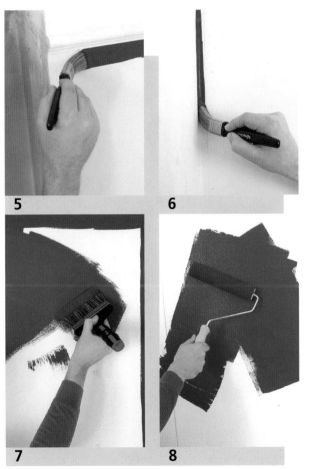

5

6

7

8

The next stage is mastering your techniques. The way you apply your paint is vital – never overload your brush. Before painting walls with either a brush or a roller, go around with a narrow brush to cover the edges **5**, the corners **6** and the space around light switches, etc., where a roller or larger brush won't reach without smudging. Paint one wall at a time so that you can complete the wall before the margins dry, otherwise you will be left with a hard line showing through. Use brushes and rollers in random directions when applying emulsion **7** and **8**.

1 **2** **3**

PAINTING WOODWORK

Woodwork first needs to be washed down thoroughly with sugar soap. Before painting, wipe the woodwork over with a damp cloth to remove any dust **1**. For a full-bodied finish, apply two coats of undercoat and one finish coat of an oil-based paint.

When painting a flush door, 'divide' it into eight imaginary squares and paint them systematically, working from top right to bottom left.

With a panelled door, paint the mouldings first **2**, then the panels, and finally the top, sides and edges. Apply primer, undercoat or gloss, by brushing in the direction of the grain, 'lay off' across the grain **3**, and finish with the grain before reloading the brush and moving on to the adjacent area. Take care not to overload the brush when using gloss paint.

TAKING A BREAK

When you take a short break, just wrap foil or cling film around the roller pile **4** or bristles **5**. Remove the foil or film when you return and the tool is ready for use once again. Overnight, suspend brushes used for oil-based paint in white spirit or paint cleaner, with the bristle tips 25mm (1in) clear of the base of the jar where sediment collects **6**. Next day, work the brush over clean brickwork or a timber offcut so that the bristles are 'dry' before starting work again. Brushes and rollers used with water-based paint can be cleaned with water, squeezed as dry as possible, then wrapped in brown paper.

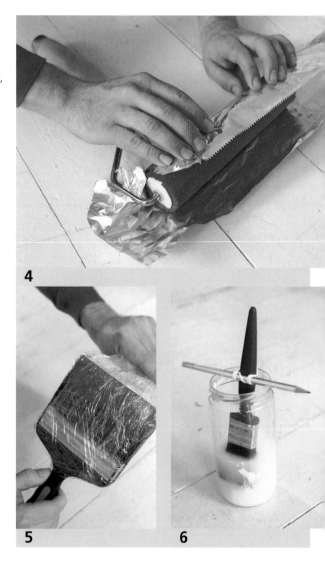

4

5 **6**

living spaces
planning

Renovating and restoring period features is a pleasing experience. Any changes or modifications you make should reflect your personality and the character of the building. Beware – extreme changes severely reduce the sale potential of your home.

renovating & design

The hardest part of renovating a house is knowing where to begin, but whether you are faced with a fairly simple task or something much more ambitious the same approach to the work involved is needed. To ensure the result you want and to avoid any disasters, the whole job has to be planned properly. Money is also a determining factor in any home improvement scheme, so make sure you work out what you can afford from the start.

MAKING A GOOD START

Before you begin any work, you need to have a clear idea of your requirements and establish your priorities, and you need to make sure the end result is comfortable and practical as well as aesthetically pleasing. For each room, start by asking yourself questions about your lifestyle.

● Who will use the room – will it be for children's use or will it be an adults-only environment?

● How will the room be used – does it have to be able to accommodate several activities or functions?

● When will the room be used most – during the day, evenings only, or just for entertaining?

CONSIDER YOUR LIFESTYLE
assess each room

Draw up a scaled plan on graph paper and mark in the fixtures such as windows, doors, alcoves, electrical sockets, telephone or television points. You can then experiment with the layout and visualise problems that may arise.

take a critical look at the room itself

● Don't expect to come up with a detailed plan overnight. The best plans usually evolve slowly, so take your time and consider each idea carefully, especially if the renovation work involved is complex.

● What do you like most and least about the room? Don't forget to consider the practicalities of electrical fittings and storage as well aesthetics such as natural light or the view from the window.

● Which features would you like to accentuate and which would you like to disguise? Answers to these questions will help to determine specific materials or jobs that may need to be done to achieve your goal.

● What fixtures and furnishings are to be retained? Make a note of their size, colour and style as they will form the basis of any new design.

make an action plan

Once you have a basic idea of what you want to achieve in each room, make a list of all the jobs that need to be done, starting with those that involve the most mess and disruption:

● Structural alterations; extension or alteration of services such as lighting (see pages 14–25).

● Replace features that need to be changed, like doors, built-in furniture (see pages 98, 102–107), shelving (see page 90) and curtain track (see page 92).

● Replace electrical fittings, fit tiles, wall panelling, lay flooring (see pages 83–84).

● Strip floors (see page 80), wallcoverings (see page 44) and old paintwork.

● Make good any damage to walls, floors or ceilings (see pages 37–39), and clean up and wash down paintwork ready for decoration (see page 52).

● Paint (see pages 50–51) or paper the ceiling and walls (see pages 44–49), and paint woodwork (see page 52).

MAKE A MOOD BOARD

A mood board will help you to create a cohesive room scheme, so once you have an idea of the look you want to achieve, start collecting colour samples, swatches and cuttings from magazines or brochures. A big pinboard is ideal for creating a mood board, but it is worth making a mini-version on card to take with you when you go shopping for accessories.

➤ For your starting point, use a picture of a room that appeals to you. Fix it in the middle of the board, then pin samples of all the elements in the room around it. Use samples in a size that reflects their proportions as they appear in the room.

➤ Walls are usually the biggest area, so have a large sample of the paint colour or wallpaper, to give an idea of the impact it will make. Actual paint colours can look different to colour charts, so it's a good idea to buy a tester pot and try it out on paper.

➤ Ask for fabric samples that are big enough to show the pattern repeat and try to obtain small pieces of flooring, as shop samples are usually too large to use.

➤ Cut out pictures of furniture and accessories that have caught your eye and add those too.

➤ If your initial collection of samples doesn't work, keep experimenting with different combinations until you hit upon the look that feels right for you.

hallways

The hall is the first impression that anyone will get of your home, so make sure that it is welcoming and, above all, has a life of its own. All too often, people treat their hall merely as a transit area to the rooms beyond.

MAKING A GOOD IMPRESSION

Clever use of colour can open up a small hall or make a large one feel more welcoming. Other rooms may be in view so the colour you choose should also complement them. Although period homes can cope with classic deep greens, navy and burgundy, dark colours tend to sap the life out of most hallways and soft, fresh colours are a better choice. Warm yellows with cream and touches of terracotta will create an inviting atmosphere in gloomy

halls, while pastel blues and green are very effective in light and airy spaces. Busy patterns make a small hall feel claustrophobic, whereas simple decorative mouldings in harmonizing shades **1** will add interest but keep the overall effect neat. Remember that decoration in halls is easily damaged – sticky finger marks, knocks and chips, etc – so choose durable finishes for the walls. Dado panelling is exceptionally hardwearing **2**.

1

2

3

4

FLOORS

Halls see more through traffic than any other area of the home, so flooring needs to be durable and easy to clean. It also needs to work well with the flooring of rooms that lead off the hall **3**, rather than create jarring contrasts. Hard materials such as ceramic and terracotta tiles suit most styles of home **4**, while solid vinyl and linoleum also create hardwearing, easy-care finishes. For a warm look without carpet, wood and wood laminates are ideal, while cushioned vinyl is a practical choice for family homes with young children. Carpet needs to be in a serviceable colour with a stain-resistant finish – small geometric patterns mask both dirt and wear and are a good solution for small areas. Durable natural matting such as coir or sisal is also a good choice. In older houses, the floorboards may be worth exposing, softened with rugs **5**.

5

STAIRS

Open plan staircases have a distinctive style that usually only needs a coat of varnish to bring out the best, but on standard staircases treads are often characterless and always noisy. Fitted carpet **1** or a natural matting will transform stairs with colour and texture, but if the treads are in good condition consider painting or varnishing them and fitting a stair runner instead **2**. Most staircases are also uninspiring, but careful choice of decorative finishes can go a long way to make the structure look more stylish. A richly polished handrail, for instance, contrasts beautifully with painted spindles and stair treads, while a chrome handrail looks fabulous with blonde wood or metal spindles. Alternatively, you can replace spindles (see page 75) and handrails, while a DIY staircase system can totally transform a hallway for a few hundred pounds.

WINDOWS

To benefit from as much natural light as possible, either leave windows undressed **3**, or try to dress them simply with as little fuss as possible – lace panels, muslin and a valance or swirls of voile on a pole are all good choices. If windows are overlooked or you don't like the view, adhesive film (see page 119), venetian blinds (see page 95) or shutters (see page 96) will afford light and privacy, while stained glass looks fabulous in halls. The real thing can be expensive, but is easily simulated by applying a specialist window film.

LIGHTING

A hallway needs a combination of good directional light, so that stairs can be used safely, and subtle ambient light to create an inviting atmosphere. Shaded wall lights, uplighters or ceiling fittings with opaque shades that throw light up on to the ceiling all provide a good level of background illumination without glare, while a table lamp or accent lighting will create warmth. For contemporary halls, consider recessing tiny halogen downlighters across the full expanse of the ceiling and illuminating every third or fourth step with a light set low into the adjacent wall. Alternatively, you can set uplighters into the treads themselves **4**.

1

2

3

4

STORAGE

Hanging space, at the very least, is needed in a hallway for coats and umbrellas, and in a family home extra storage may be useful for school bags and sports equipment – but do try to store bulky items out of sight, a curtain to draw will hide most things **5**. Put understairs space to good use: a built-in cabinet, full height cupboard or even a box seat with lift-up lid will provide plenty of storage and help to keep the hall clutter-free.

6

A traditional hatstand is still one of the best ways to hang up coats without taking up too much floor space. Wall-mounted contemporary versions of the old classic are also available, while Shaker-style peg rails are another alternative. Furniture also helps to give a hall its own identity but avoid chunky pieces that consume limited floor space. A slimline hall or console table **6** provides a place for telephone, post and keys, or you can wall-mount the phone and fix a narrow shelf to the wall underneath.

5

living rooms

Main living areas are busy places and often serve more than one purpose, acting as a play space, dining room and study, as well as somewhere to relax. So before the lids come off the paint pots it's important to consider your needs carefully.

MAXIMIZING OPTIONS

Obviously, seating will be your first priority. The chances are that this will relate to where the television is, but even in an average-sized room there will probably be two or three ways in which furniture can be organized. Arranging furniture to create discreet zones for different activities will bring a sense of order and make a room look more spacious. Consider likely traffic routes – from door to sofa, from sofa to audio equipment – and aim for a layout that allows people to move around with ease **1**.

INTERIOR ALTERATIONS

Once you've worked out the seating arrangements, you can think about where you want to install audio-visual equipment and lighting, and determine whether the existing electrical sockets are in the right place. A tangle of trailing wires is unsightly as well as dangerous, so plan for extra sockets if necessary. Lighting is also more versatile and user-friendly if it is controllable – a separate circuit for table lamps and accent lighting offers the ultimate control, but even a simple dimmer switch is a good investment.

If you plan to open up an old fireplace or install a new one, either as a source of heating or simply a welcoming focal point, you need to consider your options early on. Even if your house doesn't have a chimney, modern gas and electric appliances mean that every home can have a glowing fire, and unless you are undertaking a restoration project there is no need to be slavishly faithful to the age of the property in the design you choose **2**. Keep in mind the overall character and dimensions of the room and choose a style and size of fireplace that won't overpower it or look insignificant.

1

2

DECORATION

Colour is the first thing that you notice on entering a room and the effect can be felt as well as seen. As a general rule, neutral colours are a good bet for a living room, but if you want some colour, pastels **3** will reflect light and add just enough warmth without overwhelming a small room, while a few spicy accessories will liven up a basic 'coffee and cream' colour scheme. Deep shades and

5

3

dark colours can look gloomy, so use strong colours for accent only, although in a separate dining room, occupied mostly at night, you can afford to be much more adventurous **4**.

WINDOWS

A sitting or dining room is the best place to experiment with a grand scheme, especially if it has large windows. Window dressings can be costly, but don't skimp on fabric or it could spoil the end result – far better to be generous with a cheaper fabric than mean with an expensive one. Lace panels, sheer voiles or a simple roller blind can be used to provide privacy without having to disturb carefully arranged or tied-back drapes. For a more contemporary feel, keep curtains simple – plain fabrics hung from poles with tab, ring or clip headings look fashionably neat and can be closed easily. Alternatively, forgo curtains altogether and opt for a blind – roman blinds look particularly at home in a sitting room or dining room **5**.

4

1

Overhead light is often too harsh for sitting rooms and casts gloomy shadows. Wall lights, especially uplighters, produce a comfortable background light that creates subtle contours on walls and ceilings; in contemporary rooms, spotlights can be used. Recessed downlighters will illuminate the whole room with pinpoints of light or form accent lights to highlight foliage, a picture or a sculpture. Table and floor-standing lamps boost light levels and provide lighting for reading **3**, while lights secreted in a glass cabinet or behind a pelmet create atmosphere. In eating areas, the focal point should always be the table **4**. Sparkling glass fittings look fabulous over a formal dining table, but a rise-and-fall fitting will provide an intimate, glare-free pool of light.

2

FLOORING

When choosing a floor covering for a living area, consider comfort and how easy it will be to keep clean, as well as the style. Easy-care alternatives that can be just as comfortable underfoot, though not quite as cosy, include wood, wood-look laminates, cork and linoleum, all of which adapt well to both traditional and modern settings and look wonderful with rugs. Old floorboards may also be worth renovating **1**.

If warmth and comfort underfoot are your priority, carpet **2** is hard to beat – but make sure it is hardwearing and a colour that masks dirt. For durability, the best choice is an 80:20 wool/synthetic blend, while a 50:50 mix is a good compromise between quality and cost. In a dining room, a stain-resistant synthetic pile will shrug off spills.

LIGHTING

Living rooms need a variety of lighting: gentle ambient light for overall comfort, pools of concentrated task lighting and accent lighting to give depth and character.

3

4

5

DISPLAY

Living rooms have many different functions and you need to consider exactly what these are before you can begin to provide suitable storage. The most versatile solution will probably be a mix of open and enclosed storage; if space allows, this can be provided by one large-scale unit.

Look for furniture that will make the most of the space from floor to ceiling, and ideally offer both drawer and cupboard space as well as shelves **5**. An alternative is to buy or build one or two pieces of purpose-designed furniture – perhaps to hide away less attractive audio-visual equipment and unsightly wires – and provide shelving elsewhere for smaller items. Freestanding shelving is ideal if you like to rearrange the furniture every so often and it can double as a room divider in an open-plan living room or lounge-diner, while modular units will enable you to create exactly the storage you want **6**. Adjustable shelving is very versatile and can be used for almost anything, but as a general rule only decorative or frequently used items should be kept permanently on show **7**.

An alcove or the recesses on either side of a chimney breast are ideal places to build in a cabinet or install a bank of shelves, while even the smallest wall space can provide somewhere to display your treasures, whether it be a collection of *objets d'art* or your CDs.

In a living room that doubles as a dining room, specific storage will be needed for that role too. A sideboard is an obvious choice for housing tableware, cutlery and glasses and it can also be used as a serving table when you are entertaining.

In family homes where there are young children, life will be much simpler if you provide on-the-spot storage for toys so that they can be easily and quickly tidied away at the end of each day. A capacious chest or ottoman won't look out of place and can double as an extra seat when needed.

6

7

adult bedrooms

Although you spend comparatively little of your time in the bedroom, it's the one place you can truly call your own. Here you should feel completely at ease, so don't be afraid to indulge yourself. Make sure that the room is a reflection of your own taste and personality and a place where you can switch off and relax.

CREATING A PERSONAL SPACE

The design of the bed will stamp its style on a bedroom and the bed itself will take up a considerable amount of the space. Try to ensure that there will be enough room to walk around it and plan where storage will go in relation to the bed. For comfort, buy the biggest bed you can afford but ensure that the design is in proportion to the room and doesn't overwhelm it. Where space isn't an issue, ornate beds and those with heavy, dark frames can make a striking style statement **1**, but in smaller rooms head and footboards tend to fragment the space. Exceptions are contemporary designs in painted metal and brushed steel that are so elegantly understated they manage to maintain a streamlined look **2**. If you have a choice as to where the bed can go, consider the view as you walk into the room – the larger the area of floor visible, the bigger the room will seem **3**.

1

2

3

4

5

6

DECORATION

In theory, a bedroom colour scheme should be restful, but how you achieve this will depend on your personal taste. For some this will be achieved with a palette of cool, understated colours **4**, for others with a rich, cocoon-like canvas of warm shades **5**. The key to comfort is to use a single sweep of colour around the room **6**, so there are no visual interruptions to jar the senses, and to keep the colour of curtains or blinds similar to that of the walls.

1

2

3

4

STORAGE

Space that is free from clutter will establish a mood of calm. The simplest way to provide lots of bedroom storage is to enclose one end of the room with wall-to-wall wardrobes **1**, which can be customized to suit your needs. Allow an internal front-to-back measurement of 600mm (24in) for fitted wardrobes with enough space for doors to open easily. In small rooms **2**, neat bi-fold doors may be a better choice, whereas sliding mirrored doors will minimize the impact of the structure and make the room seem bigger by reflecting light. If you prefer separate pieces of

5

bedroom furniture, look for individual items that provide the right combination of hanging and folding space for all your clothes and shoes **3** and **4**.

FLOORING

Flooring in adult bedrooms usually gets very little wear so you can afford to economize and know that your choice will look good for years. Pure wool feels great underfoot but a carpet with a soft synthetic fibre like polyester will feel just as sumptuous for less cost **5**. Wood laminate with rugs is another good choice. Painted floorboards have an artless quality that opens up a space.

LIGHTING

Accent lighting creates atmosphere and a feeling of comfort, so it is especially important in a bedroom. Wall lights are bright enough for dressing by and provide a more pleasing light than ceiling fittings, but bedside lamps will be needed to create restful pools of light for when you want to relax **6**. You will also need good directional lighting by a dressing table or mirror. If you like to read in bed, shaded wall lights fixed about 750mm (30in) above mattress level will provide good illumination.

6

children's bedrooms

Unlike adult bedrooms, a child's room is a place where he or she will spend a great deal of time, so it needs to be adaptable to cater for multiple daytime activities as well as night-time sleepovers. From about the age of five, children will begin to show a distinct preference for certain colours and it is important to involve them in the decorating decisions.

MORE THAN A BEDROOM

Keep in mind that this is your child's room and if it isn't to your taste, then comfort yourself with the thought that in a relatively short time he or she will have outgrown it.

DECORATION

So that you do not have to redecorate at every stage of your child's development, stick to a background of plain colour that can be easily updated and resist expensive themed bedding and accessories **1**. While you may feel more at home surrounded by neutral colours or soothing pastels, children get a greater kick out of stimulating colours and patterns.

Gender specific designs – ballerinas or footballers – quickly date, so instead opt for bold checks, stripes or spots. Peel-off borders and stick-on motifs are ideal for jazzing up plain walls, while luminous shapes create a wonderful 'night sky' on the ceiling. Try to include somewhere that young artists can express themselves –

1

2

3

4

transform an area with blackboard paint **2** (and see page 114), and for older children turn this area into a pinboard.

Window treatments are also best kept simple so that expensive replacements aren't needed each time the décor changes. Blackout blinds are useful in rooms where the early morning sun intrudes upon sleep.

SHARED ROOMS

In a shared room each child should feel that they have their own space. Using one colour for two adjacent walls and a contrasting colour for the others, each with bedding to match, is a simple way to give a child his or her own 'corner' without fragmenting a small room. In larger rooms, furniture can be used to form a partition. Modular cube storage systems are ideal or you could hang a large, colourful fabric screen from the ceiling so that it can be raised or lowered as required.

FLOORING

Children's bedrooms usually double as a playroom, hobbies area or a place to entertain friends, so the floors need to be warm, comfortable and, above all, easy to keep clean **3**. A carpet with a short synthetic pile is easy-care, but carpet tiles, rubber, cork or cushioned sheet vinyl provide a smoother surface for play; remember that small toys tend to get lost on highly patterned surfaces. Older children and teenagers may prefer a more grown-up treatment with 'metallic' or funky printed vinyl tiles (see page 115). Wood laminate (see page 84) is easy to clean but can be noisy and create echoes, so it should be softened with rugs.

LIGHTING

Make sure that everywhere is well lit, especially for older children who use their room as a study. Spotlights fixed to the wall and adjustable desk lamps are a good solution. Clamp-on spotlights can be moved around as needed. In toddlers' rooms, make sure all fittings are tamper-proof – touch-sensitive lights are a safe choice – and that bedside lighting can be dimmed to a low level when required. It is now possible to buy radiator covers for children's rooms with a cutout pattern that can be illuminated by a night light after dark **4**.

the home office

Had enough of that daily commute? Well, with the creation of an office, or a well-planned office area, it may not be necessary to go into work every day – or ever again! Modern technology means that many of us can now perform a large part of our work from home.

FINDING YOUR WORKSPACE

A home office can mean workspace tucked away in a guest or master bedroom, or in the corner of a sitting or dining room. Alternatively, there may be space somewhere else in your home – perhaps in a hallway or on a landing – that can be adapted. Even a large cupboard or alcove fitted with high-level storage and a pull-out desktop or computer station could provide a suitable place to work.

PLANNING THE LAYOUT

Ideally, a desk should be near a window **1** and within easy reach of power and telephone sockets. Overloaded sockets and trailing cables are dangerous so if necessary install extra power points for your needs.

Good lighting is essential. To avoid eyestrain it should come from directly above or either side of your computer. Boost the background illumination from overhead fittings with task lighting provided by adjustable desk lamps or clip-on lamps that can be moved as required. Halogen gives a crisp, clear light that is perfect for work areas.

Wheeled office chairs are easy to manoeuvre but castors soon damage the carpet. Smooth flooring, such as hardwood, laminates and solid vinyl or carpet tiles are a better choice as they can be replaced when necessary.

Adjustable blinds are a neat solution to dressing office windows **1** and help to maintain the impression of space and order around a working environment.

STORAGE

Carefully planned storage makes it easier to keep an office area organized and tidy, and prevents it spilling over into the rest of your home. Work out your needs, then plan suitable storage using all the space available, including the walls **2**. Modular mobile storage units can double up as a desk extension or a base for communications equipment, while open shelving is very versatile. As well as ready-made storage systems, you can improvise by using wicker baskets and stackable bins. Recycled household items are easily upgraded with spray paints, while old box files can be given a new lease of life with leftover wallpaper, fabric or sticky-backed plastic. A pinboard is a practical way to keep track of messages and appointments.

FUNCTIONAL FURNITURE

Providing ample desk space at a comfortable height is the main priority. As a general rule, aim to create the largest workspace you can – a desk should be at least 500mm (20in) deep and wide enough to offer 450mm (18in) of space on both sides of your computer. A desk with a

1

2

pull-out keyboard shelf and a monitor shelf will leave precious desk space free, otherwise you'll need to allow an area 600mm square (24in square) for these two items, while a curved workstation makes good use of space in corners **3**. Desks that incorporate shelves allow printer, fax and scanner to be close to hand, but keep the desktop clear **4**. Custom-built furniture often makes the best use of awkward spaces and a desk can easily be created as part of a run of fitted cupboards. A folding trestle table is another option, but don't be tempted to make do with a kitchen or dining room chair – a proper office chair is essential if you are going to be sitting for a length of time.

DUAL-PURPOSE ROOMS

Choose office equipment that looks at home with the rest of the room and keep it neat, storing non-essentials out of sight. Workstations on which you can close the doors are ideal for combined live-and-work areas like sitting rooms, while a dividing screen is a stylish way to hide an on-view office at the end of the day. A dual-purpose bedroom needs to be organized into two distinct areas so that a quick tidy is all that is needed to allow it to be used for the other purpose. In larger bedrooms, fitted furniture ensures that sleep and work areas blend well but can be adapted to provide the two functions **5**, while in guest rooms a fold-away or raised bed leaves floor space free.

3

4

5

USING AN ALCOVE

Depending on the size of your alcove, you can put a 'hide-away' workstation here – that is, one that completely closes up to look like a cupboard when it is not in use. Alternatively, you could line the alcove yourself, to create a flat desk space with shelving above **1**. You will be restricted by the depth of the alcove for the desk support on one side, but you could angle the work surface out from the alcove and use a longer support on the side wall.

1

UNDER THE STAIRS

The space under a staircase is often under-used, but could be ideal for a small working area. Many houses have panelling under the stairs to create a cupboard, but this is always awkward to use and you could be better off without it, opening up the space and making it usable **2**. Most of the timbers under the stairs will be there only to support this panelling, so they can be removed safely. However, before you rip everything out, check that there is not a supporting timber directly under (and almost certainly part of) the upstairs newel post. You cannot take this out without providing alternative support, so take advice from a professional builder if that is what you find.

👍 **TOP TIP If you find the gas and electricity meters are in the way, you can ask the relevant utility company to re-site them for you, but it is usually easier just to conceal them in a purpose-built cupboard. If the underside of the staircase is exposed, cover this with plasterboard or plywood screwed in place so that you can easily get at this area for any necessary repairs.**

No one makes computer workstations specifically for fitting under staircases, but you should be able to find one that will fit without modification. You may still be able to add some shelves either side or above if there is space. There are companies that will make bespoke workstations to fit in any awkward areas **3**.

2

3

living spaces
downstairs

Downstairs is the area most scrutinised by curious visitors! As it will receive the most use in the house, extra maintenance is required.

staircases

Staircases are a great indicator of the build quality of a house. The grander the house, the more detailed the staircase. The reason? Once inside, the staircase is one of the first features you see, so it is important to make a good impression.

COMMON PROBLEMS

A well-maintained staircase not only looks better but it is safer to use. Most repairs are fairly straightforward but improvements may prove trickier. The most likely fault with stairs is that they creak as you walk on them. This is caused by loose parts and is most easily cured by working from underneath the stair (assuming you have access to it via an understairs cupboard) to re-secure the triangular wooden blocks between tread and riser.

SQUEAKING STAIRS

Noisy stair treads are caused either by the wood rubbing tightly together or by simple wear and tear. Sometimes,

simply puffing a lubricant such as talcum powder into a squeaking joint will cure the problem, but if it doesn't, you'll have to try something a bit more technical.

Treads (the horizontal parts) and risers (the vertical bits) are usually reinforced by triangular blocks, which are screwed in place. If any screws have worked loose, just tightening them may solve the problem. If this doesn't work, insert thicker screws of the same length, or remove the block and refix it with wood glue **1** and the thicker screws **2**. If there are no blocks, cut some from 50mm (2in) square timber, and glue and screw them into place.

In some staircases, tapered wedges fixed both vertically and horizontally hold the treads and risers together. If they are loose or worn, remove them and clean away the old adhesive. Apply new adhesive **3**, then hammer the wedges back into place **4** – the vertical one first, then the horizontal one. If necessary, cut replacements to match the old ones.

If the joint between a tread and riser is loose, you can screw up through the tread **5** and centrally into the riser (or through the riser into the tread, depending on your staircase) to force them together by screwing. Use No 8 screws that are long enough to sink about 12mm ($\frac{1}{2}$in) into the second piece. The joints between treads and risers can also be reinforced by squeezing glue into them prior to screwing.

If you can't get underneath the stairs (or if the underside of

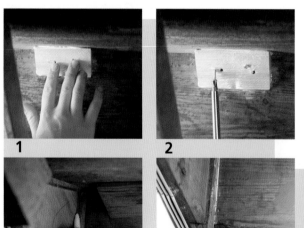

1

2

3

4

5

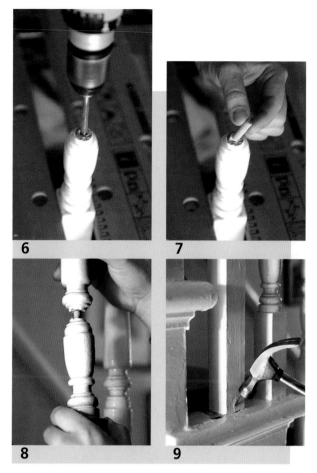

6

7

8

9

adhesive on to the top of the dowel, insert it into the hole in the upper part of the baluster, then push the two halves together **8** and leave until the adhesive has dried. To replace the baluster in position, nail through the base at an angle to secure the baluster to the tread **9**.

FITTING STAIR RODS

Stair rods are coming back into fashion. They are used only with stair 'runners' – a length of carpet running up the stairs with a space either side; they are not used with fitted carpet covering the whole stair.

Stair rods are available in brass, crystal and wood. You can order them to the correct size for your carpet. It should be emphasised that the stair rods should not be relied on to hold the carpet on their own; it should also be held by grippers in each junction between tread and riser.

Each stair rod is held in place by two brackets, one on either side of the stair runner on each tread – normally, including the floor at the bottom. Each bracket comes in two halves: you screw the bottom of the bracket to the stair after making bradawl holes **10**, lay the stair rod in the brackets and then fit the top half.

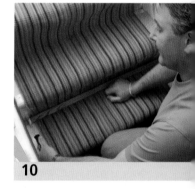

10

the stairs is covered with plaster), remove the stair carpet and drive screws down through each tread into the riser underneath, again squeezing some wood glue into the gap first. Or secure the back of a tread to a riser using L-shaped steel brackets recessed into the wood, so that both brackets and screw heads are below the surface.

If the front of a tread is loose, drill two or three holes through the front of the tread and centrally into the riser below. Use No 8 screws that are long enough to sink about 12mm (½in) into the riser.

REPAIRING BALUSTRADES

It is sometimes possible to prise apart a vertically split baluster, or spindle, and squeeze in some wood adhesive. The split can then be taped or held with a G-clamp, until the adhesive has dried. Where the split is horizontal, remove the baluster and drill small holes in the two halves **6**. Cover one end of a narrow dowel with adhesive and insert it into the lower half of the baluster **7**. Spread

adapting & changing radiators

Most halls have a radiator somewhere near the front door – and most halls need a shelf to put things down on. You can combine the two by fitting a simple radiator shelf or having a full-blown boxed radiator cover.

HIDING RADIATORS

A radiator cover is a substantial item. What it does effectively is to completely conceal the ugliness of a steel panel radiator and replace it with a styled structure, fitted with holes and grilles to allow the heat through, which can be painted or otherwise decorated in any way you want.

Most radiator covers are made from MDF (medium density fibreboard), which is easy to paint and does not rot, warp or split. Because they can reduce the amount of heat given out by the radiator, they should be installed together with reflective insulating foil fitted on the wall behind the radiator. It is essential to have a gap at the bottom of the cover to allow cold air in to be warmed by the radiator and sent on its way by convection.

You can make your own radiator cover or buy one ready made. Either way you will need to measure the radiator carefully first.

MEASURING YOUR RADIATOR

You need to take three dimensions from your radiator:
Height: from the top of the radiator down to the floor.
Width: from the outside edges of the two radiator valves.
Depth: the distance from the wall to the front of the radiator. Add 25mm (1in) to each dimension, these will be the minimum internal dimensions of your radiator cover.

A RADIATOR COVER KIT

You can buy ready-made radiator covers either from a DIY store or on the Internet through one of the specialist companies . From a DIY store, you will be choosing from a range of standard sizes, selecting a cover equal to or larger than your minimum size; from a specialist company you can also get a made-to-measure radiator cover.

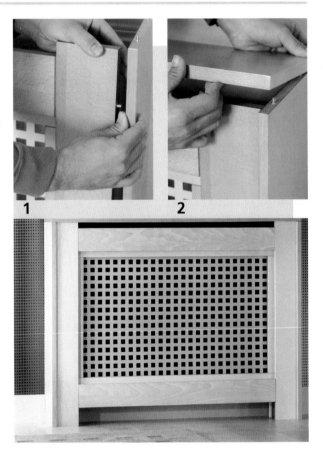

Fitting a kit is simple; you just join the pieces supplied together. Some radiator covers are simply pushed into place **1** and **2**; others, with removable or hinged panels for access to the radiator valves and bleed screw, are fixed to the wall.

FITTING A RADIATOR SHELF

As well as somewhere to put things down, a radiator shelf can be used to display pictures or ornaments which can take away from the starkness of the radiator. There are also

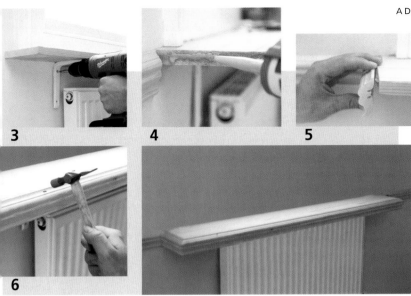

3

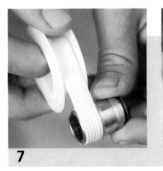

6

4

5

You could, of course, make your own radiator shelf with two wall brackets and a length of wood. A neat way to finish it off would be to run an extension of a dado rail around the shelf so that it becomes part of the decorating scheme. Place the shelf above the radiator and mark the position for the brackets. A simple tip is to fix the brackets to the shelf then fit the shelf to the wall. Screw in the shelf and first bracket **3** (use a wall plug for a solid wall). Fix the dado rail to the wall, then fit the side pieces, you will need to mitre the corners (see page 34) and glue the pieces into place **4** and **5**. Fix the second bracket, then fit the front piece to the shelf using wood glue. Finally, nail everything in place using lost-head nails **6**.

radiators that come ready-made with a seat – just right for those cold mornings! The shelf will help to direct the heat out into the room. There are several designs of purpose-made shelves available.

REPLACING A RADIATOR

7

8

9

Buy a replacement radiator the same size or width as the old one. New radiators have a much simpler hooking system than the old-style brackets. The radiator comes with two valve connectors, an air vent and a blanking plug. You need a hexagonal radiator spanner and some PTFE tape.

If you can't match the old radiator in size or style, call in a plumber to fit the replacement. Positioning new wall brackets and altering pipe runs – these are tricky for DIY.

Wrap PTFE tape round the threads on the air vent, plug, and connectors **7**, and use the hexagonal spanner to screw

them into the threaded holes in the corners of the new radiator **8**. Use an ordinary spanner to fit the blanking plug.

Lift the radiator on to the wall hooks **9** and hand-tighten the cap-nuts to connect the valves to the connectors. Tighten the nuts as described on page 26.

restoring tiled floors

If you're really lucky, you may have an encaustic tiled floor in your hallway. if not in perfect condition, it may be worth considering restoration, or it could even benefit from a thorough cleaning, as would any tiled floor, whether it be quarry or ceramic.

CLEANING AND RESTORING

One of the distinguishing features of Victorian houses can be the 'encaustic' tiled floor in the hallway, with intricate and colourful patterns. The small tiles can become loose and possibly damaged, but individual tiles can usually be replaced, provided you can get hold of suitable replacements (architectural salvage yards are a good source of second-hand tiles).

Other types of tiled flooring that may need attention are quarry tiles – widely used in Victorian kitchens and sculleries – and ceramic floor tiles, which are larger and thicker than ceramic wall tiles.

2   3

CLEANING FLOOR TILES

Floor tiles require little maintenance apart from regular sweeping and occasional cleaning with warm water and household detergent. You can buy proprietary products for removing ingrained stains, or for removing any cement stains which have been left from the installation (or repair) process. Apply the cleaner liberally with a floor mop or sponge then, wearing strong rubber gloves, use a scourer to work the cleaner thoroughly into the tiles **1**. Always follow manufacturer's instructions when using proprietary cleaning products.

1

CLEANING ENCAUSTIC TILES

If you discover the original hall tiles hidden away under the hall carpet, more often than not you will find them not only very dirty but sometimes covered in paint splashes. Fortunately, encaustic tiles are easily cleaned and any old paint can be removed with paint stripper **2** (always follow the manufacturers instructions), or with elbow grease using a scraper **3**. A good wash over with soapy water will clean off any residue. Finally, seal the tiles with a proprietary sealer.

REPLACING ENCAUSTIC TILES

Replacement encaustic tiles have to be ordered from a specialist supplier. You should be able to replace individual tiles yourself, but if major sections of the floor are involved, you may want to call in a specialist firm. Unlike other types of hard tile, encaustic tiles are laid without grouting gaps between them. The close fit helps to keep the tiles in place, but dirt and grit can build up around the edges, causing them to be dislodged and, possibly, damaged.

4

5

6

7

8

9

Individual small sections of encaustic tile may be replaced without loosening any other tiles. To remove a damaged tile, prise the piece out of the floor using an old chisel or small flat-bladed scraper **4**. Clean off any dirt and old mortar **5**. Apply a diluted 50/50 solution of PVA adhesive to the back of the loose tile and the old mortar bed **6**. If necessary, and for larger sections, cutaway the underlying mortar and lay the tiles using a cement based tiling adhesive, spread in a thin bed on the floor **7**. Replace the tile **8**, firm down and leave for 5–7 days to 'cure'. Then, if necessary, carefully sand down level with the rest of the floor, using an orbital sander or mini sander fitted with fine sanding pads **9**. This may be a good opportunity to lightly sand the whole floor area to obtain a uniform surface. I would advise sealing the floor afterwards.

FLOOR FINISHES

Glazed ceramic or quarry tiles require no further finishing. The traditional home-made finish to use on unglazed tiles is one part boiled linseed oil to three parts white spirit. This is applied with a cotton cloth, allowed to soak in and the excess removed. The finish can be improved (and its life extended) by finishing off with a coat of clear wax.

A new, or cleaned-up, quarry tile floor can be sealed using a proprietary floor sealer, applied by using a brush or roller. Tile cleaners, sealers and waxes are available from tile shops and from specialist suppliers via the internet.

wooden flooring

Timber flooring may deteriorate as the boards age and develop faults. Many faults are repairable, but sometimes one or more floorboards will need to be replaced.

REPAIRS

Over time, wooden floorboards can develop a number of faults. They may become loose, cracked or damaged, and they can develop rot. They may also warp or 'cup' (curl up at the edges), meaning they no longer provide a flat surface. All these faults need to be dealt with, whether you are keeping the floor as bare floorboards or covering it with some other material.

3

1

2

LOOSE FLOORBOARDS

A loose floorboard is likely to be noisy when someone walks over it. The cause is usually that the wood has worn and/or the nail has rusted, so that nothing is holding the board in place. Another likely reason is that a plumber or electrician hasn't fixed the boards back properly after lifting them. Either way, the answer is to pull out the nail and replace it with a screw **1** – preferably a non-rusting type like brass or zinc-plated – but only if you intend to carpet,

as it would look out of place if you sand the old boards.

PROTRUDING NAILS

As floorboards wear, the nails can sit proud of the surface. The crude method of solving this problem is to hit them with a hammer **2**, but you can easily damage the surrounding wood. It is better to use a good size of nail punch **3**, or a squared-off nail, so that your hammer blow is directed only at the offending nail.

SQUEAKY FLOORBOARDS

A squeak may occur where one floorboard rubs against its neighbours as it moves slightly when you tread on it. A simple answer is to brush some talcum powder in between the boards in the area of the squeak until the noise has stopped **4**.

4

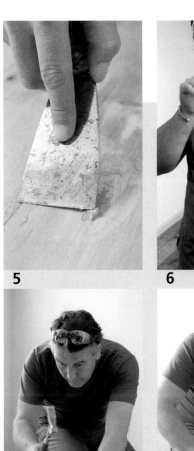

5

6

8

9

7

👍 **TOP TIP** Go to your local joinery shop or timber yard and ask them to cut the strips for you, or hire a table saw to cut them yourself. Follow the instructions carefully as table saws can be dangerous.

FILLING CRACKS AND GAPS

A split or small hole in a floorboard can be filled with wood filler or wood stopping **5**, which comes in a variety of colours. If you can't get exactly the colour you need to match the surrounding wood, mix a couple of colours together – one darker, one lighter – until you get it right. Large gaps between floorboards (which let in draughts and dust) can be filled with slivers of wood shaped to fit the gap and glued into place. For this, take up a floorboard from elsewhere in the house so that the age and colour matches the gappy floor. Cut this board into long wedge-shaped strips (see Top Tip) **6**, apply glue to each side **7** and tap into the gap with a mallet or wood block and hammer **8**. Leave overnight to dry and trim off the excess carefully with a sharp chisel **9**, then sand and polish the floor as normal, without the icy draught blowing up your trouser legs! If you want to be really clever and contemporary, you could use a contrasting timber like mahogany to make the strips!

REPLACING A FLOORBOARD

Where a floorboard has become too damaged to repair, you may want to replace it – or at least the damaged section. If you are removing the whole floorboard, you should be able to lift it up by inserting a bolster chisel and levering the floorboard, using a small block of wood as a fulcrum **1**. A floorboard will lift more easily by springing the centre of the board, rather than starting at the end. If the floorboards are tongue and groove, you will have to cut through the tongues on both sides first – with either a floorboard saw or a powered circular saw, set so that the blade just passes through the tongue but does not hit the joists below.

To remove a section, lever up a whole length, so that you can make a cut across the floorboard directly above the middle of a joist, using a floorboard saw **2**.

When you have the old floorboard up, check the width and thickness of the replacement board you need to buy. Hopefully, this will be a standard size: if the available

👍 **TOP TIP A floorboard saw is useful when working on floorboards. It has a curved blade to prevent damaging adjacent boards and the pointed toothed section on the back enables you to get into the corners.**

board is too wide, you will have to plane it down **3**; if it is too thick, you can reduce the size of the joists with a chisel or a rasp (or chisel out notches in the boards **4**), so that the board fits; if it is (slightly) too thin, place strips of hardboard or plywood on top of the joists to bring the floorboard level with its neighbours **5**. Cut the new board to the exact length.

Once the board fits exactly, drill two pilot holes to take the nails at each joist position. If the joists have a pipe or cable run across or through them, make sure any nails are well clear of these. Hammer the nails home.

STRIPPING FLOORBOARDS

Paint and varnish can be removed from floorboards using paint stripper or a heat gun. Remove old polish with white spirit and steel wool. If you intend to have the floorboards looking completely natural (with just a coat of varnish to seal them), you may have to hire a floor sander to clean them first. This is by no means an easy tool to use, so make sure you get proper instruction from the hire shop. Make

sure all protruding nails are hammered down before you start. Work through the abrasive papers, sanding at an angle to the floorboards when using coarse abrasive **6**, and in line with the boards with medium and fine. Hire an edge sander for the areas next to the skirting boards **7**.

1

2

3

4

5

6

7

FINISHING WOODEN FLOORS

The stripped, dust-free floor will need protection. For a natural-looking floor, apply three coats of clear varnish in a matt or gloss finish **A**, sanding lightly between each coat, once it has fully dried. If you do not want to go to the trouble of sanding floorboards, they can be painted with special floor paint **B**, which will cover up imperfections.

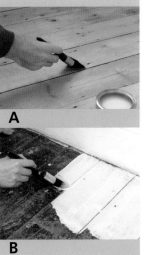

A

B

LAYING A NEW FLOOR

If your floors are too damaged to strip and you want the look of real wood but not the cost, consider a laminate floor. Modern manufacturing methods and popular demand have created a wooden look-alike floor at the fraction of the cost of a new wooden floor, However if money is not a problem, a brand-new real wooden floor is the bee's knees.

PREPARATION AND LAYING

Laying a new floor covering directly over old floorboards will eventually result in either a wonky new floor, or if you are opting for a soft flooring, there will be show-through from the old floorboards. This not only looks ugly, but the covering will wear very quickly. To avoid this happening, you need to create a smooth surface beneath your new floor. You can cover a solid floor with self-levelling compound, but for floorboards you need to install a sub-floor comprised of sheet boarding.

FITTING A PLYWOOD SUB-FLOOR

If you want to lay laminate flooring on a suspended wood floor, you must fit a 19mm (¾in) plywood sub-floor. Use full-size 2400 x 1200mm (8 x 4ft) sheets of plywood where possible. These should be butted tightly together and fixed to the floorboards with 30mm (1¼in) ring nails or screws.

Start by positioning a sheet along the longest wall, then mark the sheet in a grid fashion at 300mm (12in) spacings. Pilot-drill and countersink holes at these points so that the screws are fixed level with, or just below, the surface **1**.

Repeat this process until the floorboards are covered, staggering the sheets so that the joints do not align – this is called 'splitting the joints' **2**.

LAYING LAMINATE FLOORING

The days of gluing laminate flooring are over. Nearly all flooring now on sale just clicks together. Before installing, store the flooring horizontally in its original packaging for at least 48 hours at a temperature of 18–20°C (65–68°F).

After cleaning the subfloor you can roll out the underlay **3**. A dampproof membrane may be necessary. Begin laying in the left hand corner. Place the floorboard 10mm (⅜in) from the wall using spacers/wedges **4**. Press the end section of the next floorboard at an angle to the first one **5**, then lay it down; continue in the same manner. You will need to cut to size the final floorboard in the row. To measure, place it with the grooved end against the wall, using a spacer for the 10mm (⅜in) expansion gap, and mark where it comes up to the tongue of the previous board. Place the floorboard face down on the work surface and cut it to size using a jigsaw (or face up if using a fine-toothed hand saw). Fit to the floor using spacers.

To start the next row, use the left-over cut piece of board from the previous row; it must be at least 300mm (12in) long. Or start with a new board, cut in half. Place the floorboard at an angle against the one in the previous row, press forward and fold down at the same time **6**. To measure up the last cut row, first position a loose board exactly on top of the penultimate row, then place another

1

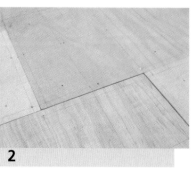

2

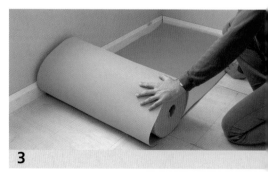

3

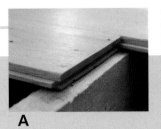

LAYING NEW FLOORBOARDS

• Check the condition of the joists for insect infestation and rot; if found, treat with preservative or replace joists entirely.

• Boards are laid at right angles to the joists with a 10mm (⅜in) expansion gap from each wall. Measure the room to calculate if you will need to cut down the width of the first and last boards. Usually you can lay a whole first row and just cut the last, but if this means the last row will be less than half a board's width, you'll need to cut both equally. With tongue and groove, cut any material off the grooved side of the first row; on the final row cut along the tongue side and then cut off the bottom of the groove so that it simply rests on the tongue of the previous row.

• Nail boards to the joists below with two nails at each joist position. Use lost head nails or floor brads at least twice as long

A

B

as the boards are thick. Lay the longest lengths you can, but where there are joins, each length must finish halfway across a joist **A**. Avoid lining up joins in adjacent boards.

• Fit each row tight against the previous row using floorboard cramps or wedges cut from offcuts **B**. With wedges, you need to temporarily fix another floorboard slightly less than a board's width away and insert the wedges into the gap. Then tap the wedges together simultaneously with two hammers in order to close up the edge joints before nailing.

---

board on top of this one but with the tongue side touching the wall; use spacers to form a 10mm (⅜in) gap. Draw a line along the edge of this top board onto the board below, and cut along this line for the required width. Fix this final row, then remove all the spacers and cover the gaps with matching beading; fix this to the skirting board, not to the floor.

DEALING WITH OBSTRUCTIONS

When laying timber floorcoverings, you may meet a pipe passing up through the floor. Mark the position of the pipe on the strip affected, cut a hole 3mm (⅛in) bigger than the pipe, then cut out a wedge from the hole to the back edge of the strip. Fit the whole piece **7** and then place the wedge behind the pipe **8**, using adhesive to hold it in

place. Where you come to a door architrave, you can either use a profile gauge to transfer the shape of the architrave on to the flooring and cut it out, or cut off the bottom of the architrave and slip the flooring underneath it.

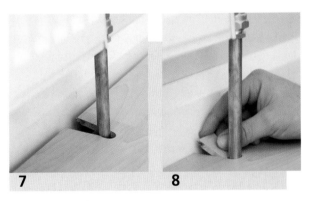

7

8

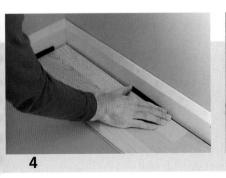

4

5

6

fireplaces

Ever since the days when fire was crucial to human survival, it has played a central part in our lives. Whether you live in a modern building or a period home, a fireplace continues to have a prominent and practical role to play – it should still be considered 'the centre of the home'!

A NEW FIREPLACE

An attractive fireplace makes a living room welcoming. Whether you want to renovate a fireplace that has been blocked off or replace a surround that doesn't match the decor, there are plenty of designs to choose from – or you could build your own. If your house has no chimney, it is possible to install a gas fire with a convincing surround.

OPENING UP AN EXISTING FIREPLACE

If you are lucky, the old fireplace you want to open up will simply have been covered over with plasterboard, the fireback will still be in place and sound, and the chimney will be clear. The worst scenario is to find the opening bricked up, the fireback missing or damaged, and the chimney capped. It is probable, however, that the original constructional hearth (the strip of concrete in front of the fire opening) will still be in place.

You can usually assess how the fireplace has been blocked up by removing the small ventilator that should have been fitted and shining a torch up. Lift the carpet in front of the old fireplace to establish the presence, or otherwise, of a hearth. From outside the house, you can

see if anything has been done to the pots on top of the chimney stack.

If, after a preliminary inspection, you wish to continue, rip off the plasterboard or remove the bricks. Starting at the air vent, clear out all rubble in the opening and brush down the

fireback to see what state it is in. Once you have opened up a fireplace, have the chimney swept. You may need a specialist to replace the fireback; have a a smoke test carried out to check the flues, too.

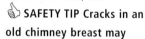 **SAFETY TIP Cracks in an old chimney breast may allow toxic fumes to enter the house, so if you are planning to have an open fire, arrange to have a smoke test carried out. To avoid the risk of a chimney fire, have the chimney swept annually.**

NO CHIMNEY?

Many modern houses are built without a chimney, but it is still possible to install a coal-effect gas fire, complete with fireplace surround. This is achieved by means of a balanced flue, a two-part duct that goes through an outside wall: one part of the duct allows the toxic flue gases to escape from the fire, the other part lets in fresh air for combustion. Normally, the flue passes straight out of the back of the gas fire through an outside wall behind. If you want to install the gas fire on an inside wall, you can buy a fan-assisted flue that can be taken via ducting to a suitable outside wall up to 7m (23ft) away.

SAFETY TIP By law, any gas fire must be installed by a properly qualified gas installer who is a member of CORGI. It should not normally be necessary to provide any additional ventilation in the room, but the CORGI installer will be able to assess this for you.

RENOVATING A FIREPLACE

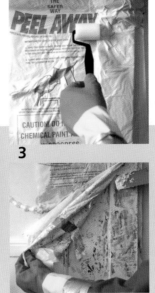

1 **2** **3** **4** **5**

Where an existing fireplace just needs a bit of cleaning up, its construction will dictate the way you do this.

Cast iron Most of these fireplaces have been painted over and it's worth going to the effort of stripping the paint off. The easiest way is with a peel-away stripping system, a paste which is spread on the surface with a scraper or the tool supplied **1**. With irregular surfaces you will need to use a brush to force the paste into crevices and grooves **2**. When you have covered the area, apply the 'blanket' and press it down with a sponge roller **3**. Slowly remove the blanket 24 hours later, and all the layers of paint will be easily removed **4**. The revealed surface should then be thoroughly washed down with warm water and rubbed down with wire wool. Finish with a pewter polish, which is a shiny silver-grey colour, and rub the surround with a soft cloth for a lovely shine **5**.

Timber surrounds Keep natural wood surrounds looking good by varnishing or treating them with a good-quality wax polish. If they have been clumsily painted, apply a blanket paint stripper so that it pulls off all the paint in the decorative detail. Scrape out the final areas with wire wool and white spirit then apply varnish or polish. Fill dents or cracks with wood filler or stopping in a matching colour.

Marble surrounds Wash down the fire surround and polish with a chamois leather. If the marble is badly stained, buy a specialist marble cleaning agent from a fireplace shop and apply it, following the manufacturer's instructions. Such cleaners are designed to penetrate the natural marble without damaging the surface. Surface scratches can be removed with a special carborundum stone (a 'slip'); small chips can be filled with a 'putty' made from china clay and two-part epoxy adhesive. Rub down with fine abrasive paper when dry and touch up with marble lacquer. Use epoxy adhesive to fix marble chips that have broken off.

Granite surrounds Although similar to marble, it is much harder and more impervious, therefore less likely to stain.

Brick and stone surrounds Just dust these with a soft brush. Brick surrounds can be treated with a sealer to prevent staining. Stick back any broken-off pieces of brick using a two-part epoxy adhesive; if a piece is missing, remove the whole brick, using a hammer and cold chisel, and mortar in a replacement brick. Re-point the mortar joints where necessary. Stone must be sealed or it will absorb soot.

Ceramic tiles Wash down with warm, soapy water. Re-fix loose tiles using ceramic tile adhesive and check that the grout lines are in good condition. Tiles on a Victorian cast-iron fire surround can't be replaced without removing the whole fireplace, as the tile panels fit into rebated steel frames, accessible only from the back of the insert. This can be done successfully when the insert is removed, and individual tiles can be sourced at the Tile museum at Ironbridge.

pictures and mirrors

Pictures, prints, photographs and mirrors personalise our homes, and we can use them to add interest to a boring wall or to help bring a room alive. The difference between a successful, eye-catching arrangement and a dull, random display lies in choosing the right spot and hanging the pictures in the best way. Here are a few tips to help you get it right.

ARRANGING AND HANGING PICTURES

Very large pictures make a statement and are best used on their own or to enhance a focal point, such as a fireplace. They also make a perfect accent for large furniture like sofas and sideboards but look most effective if they are no wider than seventy-five per cent of the furniture's size. Several large landscapes hung in a horizontal line create the illusion of width and make a narrow room look wider than it really is. Smaller pictures are ideal for narrow areas **1** or for hanging in groups; portrait-style frames used in

strong vertical lines, or simply hung one above the other will also bring a sense of height to a room.

Groups of pictures work best when sharing a common theme, for instance snapshots of family and friends or botanical or architectural prints. In general, symmetrical layouts look fairly formal, while asymmetrical layouts create a relaxed feel. Always try to think of a group of pictures as a single unit. A simple technique for achieving a balanced arrangement is to imagine the perimeter of the layout as

1

👍 TOP TIP Laying out all your pictures on a large table or the floor can help you visualize the end result and will allow you to play around with the arrangement until you hit upon one that works.

2

HANGING PICTURES AND MIRRORS

For light and medium-weight picture frames use single or double D-rings with picture wire or strong cord (right) and hang from a picture hook fixed to the wall with hardened pins.

For heavy or large picture frames or mirrors, use strap hangers screwed to the back of the frame and hang with wire or cord and picture hooks. If the frame is heavy, hang the loops of the strap directly on to screws fixed into the wall. Use a spirit level to ensure a mirror is straight.

If you are using mirrored glass over a large area, an uneven surface will distort the image it reflects. Lining the wall with plywood provides a firm foundation and evens out any irregularities.

Framed mirrors Use picture hooks nailed to the wall with hardened pins or large cup hooks screwed into wallplugs. Large mirrors can be suspended from a picture rail with picture wire or decorative chains, but if it is very heavy, you should fix the mirror directly to the wall with metal plates.

Frameless mirrors Fix pre-drilled mirrors with screws and washers and cover with chrome mirror caps (right).

Mirror tiles Fix in place using the self-adhesive pads supplied, but first make sure the surface is dry, clean, grease-free and stable. Correct an uneven surface by building up any self-adhesive pads that don't make good contact.

forming an invisible 'box'. The secret to hanging a picture is not to hang it too high – its centre should be at eye level or about 1.5m (5ft) from the floor. With a group of pictures, make a favourite frame centrepiece of the arrangement.

HANGING MIRRORS

As the most important consideration when hanging a mirror is the image it reflects, it makes sense to choose a view that makes an impact when you walk into the room. Large framed mirrors can create a stunning focal point **2** but to be most effective a mirror should be unobtrusive. The trick is to pick a spot where the edge of the mirror is not obvious – in an alcove or either side of a chimney breast, for example – and can be concealed by furniture, drapes or plant foliage. Unframed mirrors are ideal for this and you can buy one in a DIY store or glass merchant at a reasonable price. A range of standard sizes is available, though a glass merchant will cut any size you want. Mirrored glass 4mm (⅛in) thick is adequate for areas up to 900mm (3ft) square, but for anything larger use 6mm (¼in) thick glass.

shelving options

Putting up shelves is probably the most common DIY job – and often the most disastrous! This is simply because people don't use the right support for the weight the shelves will carry. You can fix shelves on to an open wall or fit them into a corner or an alcove.

CREATING OPEN STORAGE

Apart from choosing shelving that fits the bill, there are three important practical aspects to consider: the material of the shelves; the method of support; and how the support is secured to the wall. Get all of these right and you will have sturdy, attractive storage space.

1

SHELVING MATERIAL

The traditional material is solid wood, but this is expensive and usually limited to a width of 225mm (9in). The most popular materials these days are faced chipboard, with a covering of melamine or thin wood veneer, and MDF. If you want really sturdy, large shelves, you could use plywood or blockboard sheet, having it cut to whatever size you want **1**. Plywood looks good if it is well sanded and varnished.

METHODS OF SUPPORT

For an open wall, there are three choices: brackets, upright metal standards with matching brackets (to give adjustable shelving) and cantilever supports. Individual brackets may be metal, wood, wrought iron or plastic. Standards and brackets are usually made from painted steel, though aluminium and wood are also available. With standards, you only need to use a spirit level once when putting up

a whole set of shelves and the shelves themselves can be individually spaced using the slots in the uprights. Cantilever supports are designed to take either 16mm (⅝in) board or 6mm (¼in) prepared (safety) glass shelving. They consist of a triangular section with a slot in it; this is screwed to the wall and the board or glass shelf pushed into the slot.

All these methods can also be used to support shelves in an alcove, but here you have the option of a wider variety of side supports. As alcove walls are rarely true, these shelves have to be individually shaped to fit their position.

FIXING TO THE WALL

For a solid wall, drill large enough holes to take a plastic wallplug, into which you drive the screws. Use an electric drill fitted with a masonry bit suited to the screw size.

Hollow (plasterboard) walls are more of a problem, especially if you are putting up bookshelves that will take a heavy load. For display shelves, you can use hollow-wall wallplugs, but for anything else you need to find the vertical timber studs (using an electronic joist and batten detector), then fix long screws directly into these. On most partition walls, this will mean having the supports 400mm (16in) apart to coincide with the spacing of the studs.

RULES FOR PUTTING UP SHELVES

Whatever type of shelf you are putting up, make sure you have enough supports. For MDF or melamine shelving, the maximum distance between supports is:

- 15mm (⅝in) thickness: 40–60cm (16–24in)
- 19mm (¾in) thickness: 50–70cm (20–27in)
- 25mm (1in) thickness: 70–90cm (27–36in)

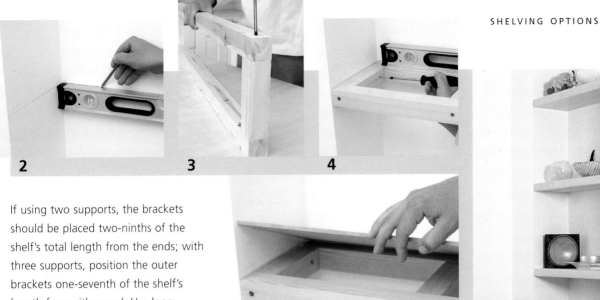

2 **3** **4**

If using two supports, the brackets should be placed two-ninths of the shelf's total length from the ends; with three supports, position the outer brackets one-seventh of the shelf's length from either end. Use long enough screws – at least 50mm (2in) No 10 and preferably No 12 gauge screws. When fixing the uprights (for adjustable shelving) on a stud wall, use 60mm (2½in) screws.

5

MAKING A LADDER-FRAME SYSTEM

My preferred type of fixed shelving is simply a made-up system fixed in an alcove, with concealed fixing positions.

Mark the shelf positions with a spirit level on all three sides of the alcove **2**. Cut two longer pieces of batten to the correct width of the shelf, then two shorter side pieces to form the correct depth when combined with the longer battens. Screw these four battens together to form the basic frame of the shelf **3**. Next, cut and fix the central support – the rear screws will have to be fixed at an angle, the front screws in the normal way. To add strength, use PVA glue at the fixing points. The shelf width determines how many central cross-supports you need (see opposite), and this is where the term ladder frame comes in. Quite simply, the wider the shelf, the more supports you need, so that the structure resembles a ladder.

Screw the frame with screws and plugs into the wall **4**. Cut the shelf boards to size, measuring from the front of the shelf to the wall, slip them on **5**, then fix with PVA glue and pins – or screw from underneath to conceal the fixing positions. Finally, to dress the front edge, use a plain wooden strip, glued and pinned or screwed from underneath the shelf for concealed fixing.

IMPROVING OLD SHELVES

If you have a plain old shelf you can easily smarten it up with special spray paint. As long as you use it in a well-ventilated room and put down lots of newspaper, this is an easy DIY project. These sprays come in many different finishes: we have used a 'stone effect' (top). Another quick effect is to use stick-on mosaic mirror tiles (below). These are simply applied with the adhesive supplied and cut and shaped to fit the shelf.

making the most of windows

Windows are often the most eye-catching aspect of a room and the feature that gives the most scope for creativity. Curtains can dress windows beautifully and the way in which they are hung can make all the difference to the overall effect.

CURTAINS

TRACKS

Curtain tracks provide unobtrusive support for curtains. As they are not designed to be on show, they are best hidden behind a curtain heading, valance or pelmet.

Plastic tracks are suitable for light to medium-weight curtains. They come in standard sizes that can easily be cut to length and can be curved to fit bow or bay windows. Tracks are available with combined hook gliders; those with concealed gliders require separate hooks but look much neater. Corded versions and two-in-one tracks with an integral valance rail are also available.

Metal tracks will support curtains of medium to heavy weight **1**. They are usually corded, telescopic and often have a central arm that neatly overlaps the edges of the curtains when closed. Steel track will support the heaviest of curtains but is suitable for straight runs only, whereas aluminium track can be shaped to suit bow or bay windows, though it is most suitable for curtains of medium weight. Curved metal tracks can be specially made to order.

Accessories Clip-on valance rails are available separately, as are extension brackets for mounting a track away from the wall, which is useful for very thick, heavy curtains.

1

POLES

Poles can be used with curtains or as the framework of more ornate treatments, with fabric draped in swags or swirled around the pole. Wooden poles are also suitable for hanging swags and tails; they will need to be either stapled or held in place with velcro. While most poles are suitable for straight runs only, designs to accommodate bay windows are available **2**.

Poles come in different materials and several sizes; the larger the diameter, the heavier the curtain it will support. As a rough guide: less than 16mm (⅝in) diameter suits nets and voiles; 16–19mm (⅝–¾in) diameter is for light to medium fabrics; 25–28mm (1–1⅛in) diameter is for medium weight and 35–38mm diameter (1¼–1½in) for medium-to heavy-weight curtains.

Metal poles come in a wide choice of designs from modern chrome and silver to traditional wrought iron **3**. They come in 19mm (¾in) and 25mm (1in) diameter. Poles over 2.4m (8ft) in length are supplied in two parts, with a joining piece. Small diameter café rods are ringless and designed for use with sheers or fitting in a window reveal.

Wooden poles are made in a choice of natural wood shades in contemporary and traditional designs **4**. Poles come in 28mm (1⅛in) and 35mm (1⅜in) diameter. Lengths of 2.4m (8ft) or more are supplied in two pieces, to be joined with a screw.

Telescopic poles have a brass-effect finish and are usually ornate and traditional in style. They come corded in 25mm (1in) and 38mm (1½in) diameters.

Accessories Many poles are now offered with a choice of complementary finials (decorative ends), which are bought separately to allow you to create your own look.

2

3

4

FINISHING TOUCHES

Pelmets and valances outline a window, defining its shape, and help to conceal any fittings, while curtain tiebacks can provide that final decorative touch.

Traditional pelmets A pelmet can be made from wood or MDF and finished with varnish or paint. A straight board 75–150mm (3–6in) deep with end returns is the simplest to construct; a box pelmet takes a little more effort and looks very stylish with a decorative scalloped edge, but this can restrict natural light.

Fabric pelmets Traditionally made with buckram (a size-stiffened cloth), the easiest way to make a fabric pelmet is to use self-adhesive stiffening that comes with a choice of design templates. Once you've cut the stiffened fabric to the required shape and length, secure it to the edge of a pelmet board with velcro fastening.

Valances Made from fabric drawn into flounces with curtain header tape, a valance creates a softer effect than a pelmet **5**. Valances can be attached to the edge of a pelmet board or hung from a valance track positioned above, or clipped on to, the curtain track.

Tiebacks A tieback holds a curtain away from a window, allowing in more light during the day. It also softens the overall effect of curtains by drawing the fabric into soft pleats **6**. Ready-made tiebacks are available in a variety of designs, including ropes and cords **7**, or you can make your own with fabric. You can also buy metal 'hold-backs' which are fixed to the wall at the sides of the window.

5

6

7

CHOOSING THE RIGHT BLIND

Blinds create an impression of neatness and space while at the same time controlling light. They work particularly well on small and narrow windows but are equally at home on big windows, and can be combined with curtains or used alone to make their own style statement. There are many types of blind and it's best to let the overall style and purpose of the room guide your choice.

Roller blinds are the simplest of all **1**. They suit all sizes of window and work well with curtains. For privacy and light control, they roll up and down on a spring mechanism. On wide windows, hanging two or three narrow blinds side by side provides greater flexibility in controlling light and shade, while perforated blinds, which allow pinpricks of light into the room, are the most versatile. Roller blinds come in a huge choice of colours and patterns as well as wipe-clean finishes and blackout material, which is ideal for a child's or night-worker's bedroom.

Pinoleum blinds are made from split bamboo or thin slats of wood, woven together **2**. They roll up and down using a system of cords secured around a wall-fixed cleat. When lowered, soft light filters through the slats and the blinds offer total privacy. Pinoleum in fashion shades is perfect for any fresh, modern interior, whereas plain bamboo has a distinctive look that is most at home with earth colour schemes, plants and natural flooring like wood or matting.

Reef blinds are made from fabric, like roller blinds, but they roll up and down in the same way as pinoleum blinds, using bold contrasting decorative ties instead of cords. The overall effect is less neat than either roller or pinoleum blinds, so they can look untidy on wide windows, but they have an artless look that gives a room warmth.

Ruched blinds pull up into soft ruffles and create the look of curtains but use far less fabric. Festoon blinds are permanently gathered into ruched swags, whereas Austrian blinds hang like a curtain when down. Both types can be hung from a track or a curtain pole, or can be fixed on a rail. Although the blinds can be washed, the folds trap dust and also obscure a large part of a window

1

2

even when raised, so they are best made from fine sheer fabrics to allow light to filter through. As the joins are visible, ruched blinds are best used on windows that are narrower than the average fabric width of 1.2m (48in).

Pleated blinds are made from stiffened polyester pressed into crisp, narrow pleats that concertina together as the blind is raised with cords **3**. They come in plain colours or simple patterns, often with a light-reflecting finish, and diffuse, rather than block out, light when closed. Pleated blinds have a neat appearance that suits small windows and can be used for privacy with simple curtains.

3

4

Roman blinds are made with wide, horizontal pleats that fall into deep, neat folds as the blind is raised and lowered by cords **4**. The overall effect is smart and plain fabrics or vertical stripes show off the beautiful symmetry best of all. Roman blinds create an illusion of width so are perfect for tall, narrow windows and can be used on their own or with tailored floor-length drapes.

Venetian blinds come in many colours and metallic and mirrored finishes, as well as wood and wood effects. They offer complete privacy without necessarily blocking out light **5**. Many ranges offer a choice of slats – standard 25mm (1in) slats suit most windows, although 15mm (⅝in) slats look neater in small windows and chunky 50mm (2in) wooden slats are best for large windows. The slats can be adjusted to control light levels or the blinds can be drawn completely clear of the window.

Vertical blinds are made from stiffened strips of fabric, or 'louvres', attached at the top to a track and chain-linked at the bottom. Standard louvres are 90mm (3½in) or 127mm (5in) wide and pivot open and closed to control light, or can be drawn across a window like curtains. The slats can also be graduated in height and made to fit odd-shaped windows, or hung on a curved track in a bay. The semi-commercial look of vertical blinds suits contemporary homes and is best used floor to ceiling or in tall, narrow windows.

FITTING BLINDS

Blinds can be fitted outside or inside a window reveal, provided the mechanism does not obstruct the use of the window. Where modern tilt-and-turn and pivoting windows are installed, blinds should be fitted outside the reveal. If you are fitting a blind inside the reveal, measure its width at several points and use the narrowest measurement to ensure that the blind will fit comfortably within the recess.

5

INSTALLING AND REPAIRING SHUTTERS

Shutters are a uniquely architectural window treatment. In period properties, they would normally be installed in an angled reveal, but they can also be fitted outside the reveal or to lie flush to the frame, which gives definition to a window without detracting from its shape or the view.

Traditional louvred shutters offer privacy, ventilation and adjustable light. The louvres of most shutters are around 68mm (2¾in) wide, though European-style shutters have 45mm (1¾in) slats and plantation-style colonial shutters have deep 90mm (3½in) slats. Solid panelled shutters are another option and are less versatile than those with adjustable slats. Shutters can be made to fit a window's full height or be installed in panels, tier upon tier, with each one working independently, or as half-height café shutters.

1   **2**

INSTALLING SHUTTERS

Face-fixing shutters to the outside of a window allows more natural light into a room as the whole of the window is exposed and it is by far the easiest option. Shutters should overlap equally all round, with the louvres opening inside the reveal, but if the sill protrudes, fix shutters so

that the bottom edge is 3mm (⅛in) above it. Shutters can be hinged to a timber batten fixed to the wall with wallplugs and screws, or secured with offset hinges screwed into the shutter frame and wall.

If the window is square, shutters can be fitted directly to the reveal with butt hinges, although offset hinges will allow the shutters to be adjusted if necessary. If the reveal is not square, timber battens are required. If using battens either inside or outside the reveal, try to use timber that complements the shutters or paint it to match.

First make the frame, screwing the timbers at right angles to make the corners **1**. The frame should be 8mm (⅜in) wider than the shutters at the sides and the height should be the same as the shutters. Fix the frame to the window with screws and fix one half of the hinge to the face of the frame. This will cover the screws fixing the frame to the window. Fix the other half to the shutter and join the hinges **2**.

REPAIR AND RENOVATION

A drop of oil on hinges and a new set of cords may be all that is needed to restore an old set of panelled shutters to good working order. However, if you decide to strip off old paint, use chemical stripper in preference to hot caustic stripping, which can split thin panelling. Where the joints of louvre shutters are loose, carefully pull the components apart, clean up the joints and reassemble them.

living spaces
upstairs

This is the private part of our homes, where we can indulge ourselves. We often have to adapt this space to suit our individual needs, and this requires creative use of the space!

making a customised bedhead

We all like to sit up and read in bed sometimes. In order to do that comfortably you need a bedhead, or headboard, so why not make your own? A proper bedhead lends the bed a more 'finished' feel. It gives you something to lean against when reading and will help to keep the wall clean – and it has the practical advantage of stopping things falling down behind the bed!

MAKING YOUR OWN BEDHEAD

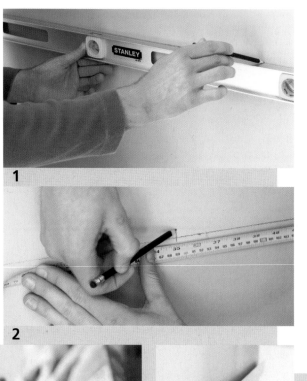

A number of materials are suitable for making your own bedhead, which can extend above the bed for anything from 300mm (12in) to 1m (3ft 3in). For a plain bedhead, veneered chipboard, plywood or MDF board are good choices; veneered chipboard needs varnishing, while MDF needs painting. MDF and plywood come in large sheets, typically up to 2440 x 1220mm (8 x 4ft); veneered chipboard comes in widths of up to 600mm (2ft). You will also need some softwood battens to attach the bedhead to the bed.

BED-ATTACHED BEDHEAD

Some beds have a pair of holes with matching bolts fixed as standard, allowing you to fit a bedhead mounted on vertical battens. You'll need to cut slots in the batten ends so that they can be slid into place when you slacken the bolts. Don't forget to tighten the bolts up again!

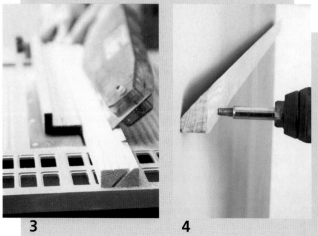

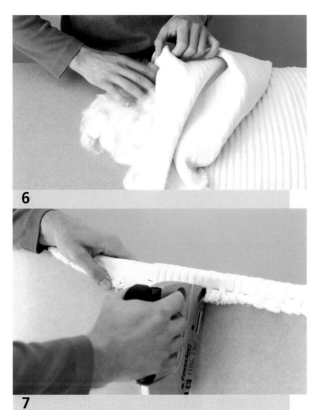

6

7

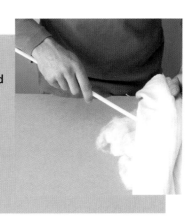

👍 **TOP TIP If you stuff the headboard using polyester filler, use a stick or rod to push it into the corners and ensure that it is compacted.**

WALL-ATTACHED BEDHEAD

This type of bedhead can be made wider or narrower than the bed. Draw a line to mark the position of the bedhead, using a spirit level to ensure the line is level **1**. Measure along the line to find the centre above the bed and mark this point **2**. Cut the bedhead to length.

You will need two battens to fit the bedhead to the wall; these could be softwood, veneered chipboard or hardwood to match the veneer of the bedhead. One strip needs to be cut into two, using a flat-bed cutter with the blade set at 45 degrees **3**, or a panel saw, making the cut at a 45 degree angle. One half of this, with its angled edge facing up, is screwed to the wall along the marked line **4**; the other is screwed to the back of the bedhead at the top, such that it wedges down into the wall-mounted half **5**. The second whole strip is fitted to the bottom of the bedhead and simply acts as a spacer to hold the bedhead vertical against the wall.

UPHOLSTERING BEDHEADS

There are many ways you can upholster a bedhead to make it more comfortable. If you want one of the more exotic finishes, such as leather or quilted fabric, get a professional upholsterer to do it for you. But if you want something simple, you can pad the bedhead with flame-retardant upholstery foam or polyester wool (as used in cushions), and cover it with fabric **6** – perhaps some spare material left over from the bedroom curtains. Fix the fabric tightly to the back of the board using a staple gun **7**.

space-saving beds

Ever had that feeling you could fall asleep standing up? Well here's your chance! If lack of space is a major factor, you might want to consider fitting a bed that folds up against the wall when not in use, as this can be a great space saver. Three simple types of 'wall bed', as they are commonly known, are fairly straightforward to install.

FITTING A WALL BED

There are three main types of wall bed. The simplest design, which is often referred to as a 'swing-away', is a plain metal bedstead fitted on a large bracket with counter-balance springs. It folds back to a depth of just 420mm (16½in) when closed, but remains visible unless you construct a cupboard around it **1**. A more sophisticated type allows you to fold the bed away into its own cupboard.

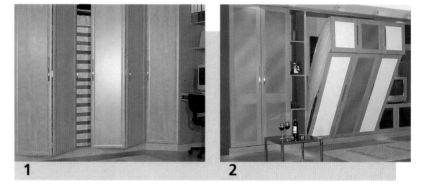

Sometimes called a 'fold-away' **2**, this has a fake cupboard door front attached to the underside of the bed, so that when the bed is raised against the wall it is completely concealed behind the door. A 'hide-away' wall bed takes the process one step further, with mock cupboard doors that show at the end of the bed when it is folded down.

All three types of wall bed are fitted with straps to hold the mattress and the bedclothes in place when the bed is folded up against the wall.

FITTING A FOLD-AWAY BED

When you buy this type of wall bed, it should come with instructions for making up the cupboard into which it fits when not it use. The cupboard needs to be solidly constructed and firmly fixed, as it will take the full weight of the bed.

Make the cupboard from 18mm (¾in) sheet material, following the instructions that will be supplied by the bed manufacturer. For the external doors, the side panels may need to be cut away and additional strengthening side

panels fitted (unless the cupboard is fitted between other secure cupboards).

It is possible to fit a bedhead to the bed, which will stop things falling down behind it and into the cupboard. This can be bolted to the bed frame, but has to be in two hinged parts with chamfered edges, so that it folds down as the bed is raised.

To finish off the job, fit the fake door to the underside of the bed frame and mount the bed bracket in the cupboard, using the bolts, nuts and brass countersink screws supplied. Finally, adjust the bed until it operates correctly and is centrally mounted in the cupboard.

FITTING A HIDE-AWAY BED

A hide-away bed is very similar to a fold-away bed, except that the cupboard has to be bigger to take the extra doors that form the bed-end when the bed is down. It needs to be at least 500mm (20in) deep, slightly wider than the bed frame and normal ceiling height – 2.3m (7ft 6in) – though the height of the main part of the cupboard must match the bed frame exactly. The doors are attached to the bed frame and the bottom (main) door is additionally secured to the base of the cupboard (that is, above the cupboard plinth), using a continuous piano hinge. If two doors are used side by side, they should be permanently joined using metal bars. Full adjustment is provided so that the bed operates correctly.

FITTING A SWING-AWAY BED

It is a very simple job to fit a swing-away bed. First screw the support bracket to the wall and floor **3**, then slot the bed frame into the bracket and tighten the bolt **4**. The bed is simply lowered into place when you want to use it, its end legs dropping down automatically **5**. The only installation problem you are likely to encounter is where the wall is a hollow partition type, rather than a solid one. Unless you can fix all the screws into the vertical wall studs (you can find these with a joist and batten detector), it will be necessary to provide additional support on the wall. The easiest way to do this is to screw a large batten – say 75 x 38mm (3 x 1½in) – to the studs and then screw the bed bracket to this. If space is so tight that you don't want to lose the 38mm (1½in) space taken up by the batten, you could cut away the plasterboard and part of the studs and recess the batten with its front face flush with the wall. Make good with plaster after doing this.

3

4

5

wardrobes

Clothes storage is essential if you don't want your bedroom to be in a perpetual mess, and a wardrobe is the obvious solution. You can buy a freestanding one ready-made or purchase an inexpensive flat-pack to assemble yourself at home. Alternatively, you could install a fitted wardrobe to make the best use of the available space.

INSTALLING FITTED WARDROBES

A fitted wardrobe can be one of three kinds: hinged door, sliding door or walk-in. All three involve making some kind of partition in front of an existing wall. In the first two types the door, or doors, form the partition, but with a walk-in wardrobe you need to build a proper partition wall with a door by which to enter.

Once you have determined the type of wardrobe you want to install, you need to decide how you will fit it out – with hanging rails, shelves, baskets, drawers and so on – and how you are going to light it, so that you can see what is inside.

FITTING A WALK-IN WARDROBE

A walk-in wardrobe has the advantage that everything is completely hidden from view and you can create a fair amount of storage space, with access to clothes on both sides. You could have a hanging rail on each side or a single rail and shelves and/or drawers on the other side.

As the minimum width for a walk-in wardrobe with hanging rails on both sides is 1.8m (6ft), you will obviously need a largish room to start with. The ideal total space would be around 2m (6ft 6in) square, and preferably in the corner of a large room, this means you'll be building two partition walls at right angles, with a door in one side.

A partition wall is normally built from 100 x 50mm (4 x 2in) sawn timber (though for this project you could use 75 x 50mm/3 x 2in timber) and consists of four elements nailed together. The floor plate runs the length of the wall and is screwed down to the floor; the ceiling plate runs the length of the wall and is screwed to the ceiling; vertical studs run between the floor plate and the ceiling plate; and horizontal noggings are fitted between the studs, about half way up but staggered (so that you can get the nails in from either side). Studs are normally spaced at 400mm (16in) centres, but for this project, a spacing of 600mm (2ft) for the unbroken wall and 450mm (18in) for the wall with the door would be better.

Check out the area. You don't want to put a walk-in wardrobe where there is a window and, ideally, you don't want to cover up any socket outlets (though you may be

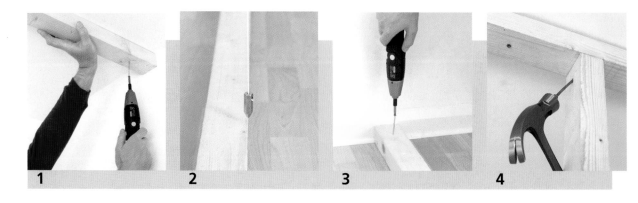

1   2   3   4

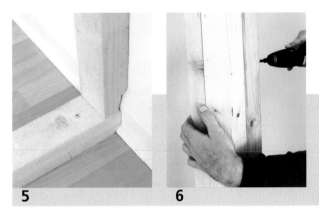

5 6 7

able to make use of the power to provide lighting in the wardrobe). Work out all the details on paper – the location of the partition walls and the door (as well as which way this will open), the hanging rails and shelving. As the partition walls need to be secured to joists, try to make one of the walls line up with a joist above and, ideally, with a joist below, though this is less important.

👍 **TOP TIP Use a joist and batten detector to find joists in the floor and ceiling and which way they run.**

Install the ceiling plates first. Cut them to length and drill and screw them to the ceiling joists above **1** (or to the noggings fitted between the joists), using long screws. Cut and fit the floor plates next, using a plumb line to make sure the floor plates are exactly below the ceiling plates **2**. Screw the plates to the floorboards **3** or, preferably, to the joists below. (You will need to cut away any carpet so that they sit directly on the floor itself.)

Mark the positions for the vertical studs and cut each one to length individually as you fit them. Hammer the nails at an angle through the sides of the timber down into the floor plate and up into the ceiling plate **4**. At the ends of the wardrobe, shape the studs to fit round the skirting (or cut the skirting away) **5**. At the partition corner, fit three studs so that the ends of both internal and external plasterboard sheets will be supported **6**.

Position the studs either side of the doorway to allow space for the door lining, which is 100 x 25mm (4 x 1in) planed timber. Check this carefully so that you will be left with the correct gap for the door – that is, the door width plus 6mm (¼in) – once the lining is fitted **7**.

Add noggins between all the studs about half way up (and, perhaps, at the height you want the hanging rails), plus a longer noggin over the doorway and an extra short stud (the 'cripple') running from the centre of this noggin to the ceiling plate **8**. Once the doorway is complete, cut away the length of floor plate within it **9**.

Fit and screw the door lining to the studs either side of the doorway **1**. It must protrude 12mm (½in) on either side in order to line up with the plasterboard. Then fix the plasterboard to the studs with plasterboard nails – grey side out if you are going to give them a skim coat of plaster, ivory side out if you intend to paint or paper them directly **2**. Each edge must be supported over a stud; fit the full sheets first, then cut sheets to fill the gaps **3**. Apply joint filler to all the joints **4**.

Hang the door **5**. You will need a doorstop for the door to close against, hinges and a magnetic door closer. To finish off, fit a light inside the wardrobe. Decorate by painting or papering the plasterboard walls and painting the door and its frame, then fit out the wardrobe **6**.

1

2

3

4

5

6

7 8 9

FITTING A SLIDING DOOR WARDROBE

Fitting a sliding door wardrobe is a lot less work than creating a walk-in wardrobe and it consists of building a frame in front of a wall to take the sliding doors. If the doors are not the full height of the wall, you will have to make a filler panel to go above them; if the wardrobe does not extend the full length of a wall (which is the ideal), you will need a filler panel or a 'return' panel to fill the space **7**. Return panels are commonly used where the wardrobe is built next to a doorway in the corner of the room: the wardrobe then extends from there to the next wall. Construct the return end panel from melamine-faced chipboard. Cut it to fit the ceiling height exactly and scribe the back edge to fit the rear wall and skirting. Fix the return end in position with blocks, equally spaced.

Full fitting instructions should be provided with the sliding wardrobe doors, but briefly the order of work will be: preparing the opening; fitting the tracks; hanging the doors; and fitting out the wardrobe.

Preparing the opening is the crucial part. Inside, the wardrobe will need to be a minimum depth of 600mm (24in) from front to back **8**. If the joists above are parallel with the track, either use the nearest joist or go to the room or loft above and fit noggins between the joists to secure the timber to. If your ceiling height is over 2.2m (6ft 6in), use spacer blocks to reduce the height. If you need to lower the ceiling, the best way is to construct a small

10 11

timber frame of the height required, consisting of two long lengths of timber joined (with screws and adhesive, not nails) by a series of small uprights. Secure the top track to the ceiling with screws – make sure it is firmly attached as it will take the weight of the door **9**.

Once the top track has been fitted, use a plumb line to establish the position of the bottom track **10**. The floor track should be positioned 32mm (1¼in) back from the front line of the top track. Fix the floor track directly on top of the floorcovering, using doubled-sided adhesive pads or screws **11**. Both tracks must be horizontal, so check with a spirit level and use packing pieces if needed to achieve this. The floor track should never be raised on a plinth as this could lead to doors leaving the tracks.

6

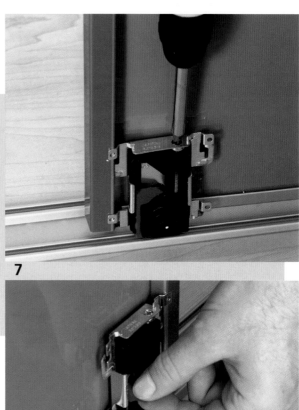

7

8

To install the doors, always locate the back door first. Install doors with the bottom of the door slanting out at 15 degrees. Lower the bottom wheels into the bottom track before engaging the top guides.

To engage the top guide, push up the white plastic section of the guide to engage in the top track **6**. Align the doors plumb to the side walls. Adjust the bottom wheels to alter the height and angle of each door. Using a Pozidrive screwdriver, correct the door alignment with the screw adjuster attached to the bottom wheel **7**. Turn the screw clockwise to lower the door and anti-clockwise to raise it. Plumb the doors to the adjacent walls and other doors by adjusting both left and right wheels up and down as required.

To ensure that the doors do not leave the tracks, the anti-jump clips should be engaged by rotating the clip into the open position, pushing it fully down into the track and rotating it back into the closed position **8**.

HINGED DOOR WARDROBES

A wardrobe with hinged doors is fitted in much the same way as a sliding door wardrobe, except that you will need substantial and well-secured uprights to take the hinged doors. The best type of catch to use is a 'touch latch', which holds the door closed until you simply press the door once to open it.

LIGHTING

There is no point in building yourself a wardrobe if you can't see what is inside it. Proper lighting is the answer and there are two sensible solutions.

One is to have eyeball spotlights fitted in the ceiling or above the wardrobe so that they shine down on to the contents once the doors are open. You (or an electrician) should be able to fit these fairly simply, using the existing lighting circuit – perhaps replacing a single central room pendant light with four ceiling spots, two of which are in front of the fitted wardrobe (see page 20–25). This solution would also work for a walk-in wardrobe, except that here you would probably want a separate light switch by the door. A simpler way would be to fit a light above the door **9**. The other solution is to fit a light inside the wardrobe itself, perhaps one that is operated by

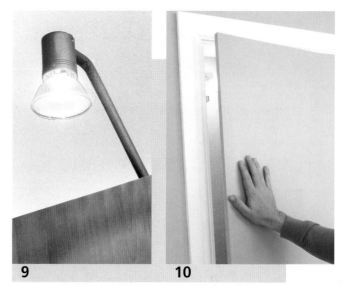

9   **10**

a push-button switch that is released as you open the door **10**. Position the light so that it is concealed and shines on the wardrobe contents when the door is open, rather than into your eyes.

FITTING OUT A WARDROBE

There is a huge variety of fittings available for the inside of your fitted wardrobe. Some may be supplied with a sliding wardrobe kit, but there are many others you could use, including the following:

➤ **Hanging rails** – usually in a chrome or white finish, and secured either to the underside of a fixed shelf or to the end walls.

➤ **Shelves** – usually fitted between the side panels, using support pegs; they can be either fixed or adjustable.

➤ **Tie rails and tie/belt holders**

➤ **Drawers and open sliding baskets** – usually fitted between the side panels, 500mm (20in) or 600mm (24in) apart.

types of storage

A clutter-free home will always feel more relaxed and look more spacious than an untidy one. Although it's true that you can never have too much storage space, you need to think carefully about the type of storage that will work and look best, as well as the amount you require.

A PLACE FOR EVERYTHING

CUPBOARDS

Cupboards are ideal for storing big items and anything you want to keep out of sight. Fixed to the wall, they can also keep floor space free **1**. If your walls are uneven, a cupboard won't sit straight, so hang one on adjustable brackets or timber battens fixed to the wall. With suitable fixings, cupboards can cope with quite weighty loads but you need to make sure that they are loaded evenly, storing the heavier items at the bottom, rather than all to one side. Ensure that the top shelf is easily accessible and the contents can be seen and reached easily.

DRAWERS

Drawers are often more convenient than cupboards because they open to give you a clear view of the contents **2**. The most versatile units are those that offer different depths of drawer. Avoid storing heavy items in a drawer, unless the base and runners are sturdy.

USING GLASS

Glass is perfect for display shelving and looks wonderful in sitting rooms and bedrooms accented by hidden lighting, while textured glass adds even more interest. Ready-made glass shelves are available in most DIY stores but if you need glass cut to size, make sure that it is toughened safety glass at least 6mm (¼in) thick. Support 6mm (¼in) glass every 400mm (16in) and 9mm (⅜in) glass every 700mm (28in); use for light loads only.

SHELVES

Wall-mounted shelving is very versatile, particularly if it is adjustable. Floor-standing shelves can be moved around as required and can usually cope with heavy loads. If unevenly loaded, a tall floor-standing unit can be pulled over, so use discreet angle brackets to secure it to the wall. Shelves less than 200mm (8in) deep are generally suitable only for display purposes or toiletries. Heavy items like books will require shelves at least 18mm (¾in) and preferably 25mm (1in) thick.

HOOKS AND RAILS

A peg rail or one with hooks and a narrow shelf offer handy hanging space for anything from coats to pairs of shoes, toys or sports gear. In children's rooms and hallways make sure the rails are low enough to be reached easily.

1   2

3

DUAL-PURPOSE FURNITURE

Invest in furniture that will do two jobs in one. A blanket box or a chest make good alternatives to a coffee table **4** or a bedroom chair. They can be used for books, bedding or bulky sweaters, while a window seat (see page 110-113) could double as a spacious cupboard.

4

OTHER TYPES OF STORAGE

Even if your home is bursting with shelves and cupboards, portable storage is invaluable for taking any overflow and for those possessions you might want to use in different rooms around the house **3**.

Baskets and bins made from wickerware, metal or cheerfully coloured plastic are perfect for big or bulky items like children's toys, maps and wrapping paper. If they are on show, choose a design to suit the style of the room.

Stack 'n' store crates are a practical choice for items you want to move from room to room, such as cleaning materials, tools or toys. Fitted with castors, they can be moved around with ease.

Boxes with lids made from heavy-duty cardboard come in a range of sizes suitable for anything from stationery to spare bedding. Hat boxes are perfect for fragile items and look decorative perched on top of a wardrobe.

Mobile trolleys are great for children's toys and those that can be customized with drawers will provide a complete storage system for paperwork or your CD collection.

Pocket organisers that hang on the back of a door are a convenient way to store toiletries or small items like gloves and tiny toys that easily get lost. The pockets on some designs are big enough to take shoes.

ORGANISING SPACE

Cupboards, drawers and fitted wardrobes are more versatile if the inside is organised to suit your needs. Fitting a second, lower rail in a wardrobe that is used only for shirts and trousers instantly doubles the hanging space, or you could take advantage of the spare space by installing a bank of drawers. Complete systems of shelf units and hanging rails are available for transforming fitted wardrobes into fully functional storage **5**. Items stored at the back of floor-standing cupboards can be hard to reach but wirework systems (designed for kitchen cupboards but no less useful elsewhere) will convert the space and bring the contents closer to you. Drawer organisers and trays ensure the contents are filed neatly and don't get mixed up; they are most useful for stationery, cosmetics and underwear.

5

making a window seat

A window seat can be a wonderful way to watch the world go by. it is a delightful place just to sit and view the outside world. You can fit one into a bay or bow window with a minimum of carpentry skills.

CONSTRUCTING A SEAT

The easiest style of window in which to fit a window seat is a square bay and the most difficult is a curved bow window, while an angled bay window comes somewhere between the two. It's not a good idea to fit a window seat in a bay window containing a radiator; although it might be nice and warm for the person sitting on the seat, the rest of the room could be significantly colder, even if you make proper airways in front of and above the radiator.

1

THE CHOICE

The simplest window seat is basically a large shelf, supported along three edges, that is strong enough for someone to sit on. With a little more effort and materials, you could build a storage box into the window recess, for example, using the sides and back of a square bay as three of the sides of the box and constructing a panelled frame for the fourth (front) side, with a hinged lid to create the seat. Another possibility is to join some small cupboards together (kitchen wall units designed to fit over a hob would be ideal), mounting them on a frame and bolting them together, then adding a flat seat across the top. The advantage of this method is that you can access the storage space under the window seat from the front rather than having to lift up a lid.

All three methods allow for the seat to be upholstered. To do this, simply glue foam padding to the seat and cover it with fabric, stapling it under the lift-up seat. You could also add an upholstered back rest above the seat so that you can lean back in comfort. If upholstering seems like too much bother, you can simply use cushions.

MAKING A HINGED WINDOW SEAT

A hinged window seat is supported on all four sides – by two or three hinges (or a full-length piano hinge), fitted at the back to a batten secured to the back wall, by two battens secured to the side walls and by a simple ladder timber frame at the front. You will need 50 x 50mm (2 x 2in) timber for the frame and the battens, and 18mm (¾in) MDF or plywood for the seat or lid and the front panel.

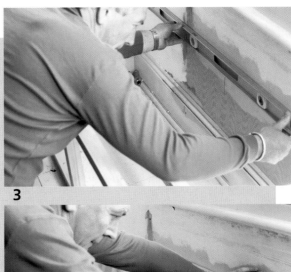

3

4

2

👍 **TOP TIP Your bay window will probably not be completely square, so measure it carefully 1. If necessary, make a cardboard template of the exact shape for the lid.**
To make the frame, first cut a length of timber to form the base, making it fit snugly between the skirting boards on the opposing sides of the window. Position it just behind the skirting corners, so that the front of the window seat lies flush with the adjacent walls. Cut the two side members of the frame to the required height and mark these R and L – they may need to be different lengths to get the top member level, so check with a spirit level. They may also need to be cut away to fit around the skirting board. Cut the top frame member to length, then cut two more verticals to fit exactly between the top and bottom pieces, spaced equally along the front. When you are happy with the frame (it may take a bit of shaping with a rasp and a chisel), join it together with screws **2**.

With the front frame in place (but not yet secured), use a spirit level to mark the position of the back batten on the wall **3**. The lid fits in front of the back batten and overlaps the front frame, hence the back batten sits higher than the front. Use a piece of the lid material to allow for the thickness of the lid. Cut the batten to length, then drill and countersink holes for 90mm (3½in) No 12 brass securing screws. Mark the screw positions on the wall, drill holes and fit wallplugs, then screw the batten in place **4**. Using the lid, mark on the back batten where the underneath of the lid will be and mark on the side wall where the battens should be **5**. Take your time to cut these square and exactly to length (it doesn't matter if they are a bit short, but the front edge must butt neatly against the rear of the front frame). Secure these battens to the side walls.

5

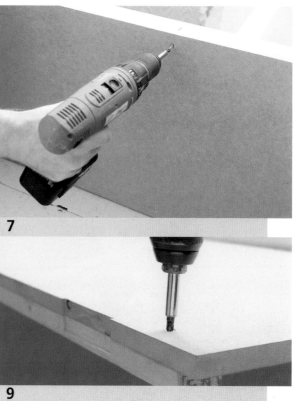

7

6

9

add plenty of cushions to make the window seat feel even more comfortable and luxurious

8

Screw the front frame to the ends of the side battens at the top and to the floor at the bottom, using 75mm (3in) screws. Screw additional battens for added strength if required **6**.

Cut a panel for the front from MDF or plywood sheet and shape it to fit around the skirting boards at the lower edges. It can be left just a fraction short of the floor, but the top edge must line up with the top of the frame. Screw the panel to the frame with 40mm (1½in) No 8 screws **7** at 150mm (6in) intervals.

Cut the lid to size, round off the front edge using a router **8**. Chisel out the recesses in the lid to take the hinges and fit a hinge-supporting batten made from 40mm (1½in) square timber along the back edge **9**. Take your time over this and use a sharp chisel, as any errors will show.

Chisel out the recesses in the back batten for the other half of the hinges **10**. Secure the lid to the back batten using three 75mm (3in) brass or chrome hinges.

A plywood seat can be varnished and brass screws will enhance its appearance. An MDF seat is best painted, and you may want to fill in the visible screw heads **11**.

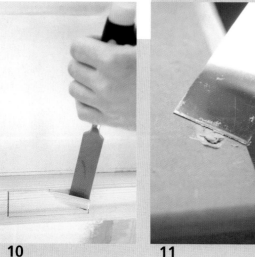

10

11

children's rooms

Often one of the smallest rooms in the house, a child's room needs clever planning if it is to accommodate clothing, toys and other possessions. It should also leave enough space for play, homework and entertaining friends – especially as most children 'store' everything on the floor!

SPACE-SAVING IDEAS

BEDS

In children's rooms, several tiers make sense. A high-rise loft bed creates space below for bookshelves and a study area, while a cabin bed provides generous under-bed storage for big toys. Bunk beds are often the only way of fitting two children into a small bedroom and are ideal for accommodating overnight guests, but they are not really suitable for children under six. If you intend to buy a conventional bed, consider investing in a guest or stowaway bed – which stores another single bed stored underneath – or a divan with drawers. For very small or awkward spaces, consider a tailor-made 'sleep-and-study' design or a stowaway bed (see page 100).

FURNITURE

While small-scale furniture and a bed that looks like a boat may be very appealing, don't forget that children's tastes change as fast as they grow, and full-size furniture in an adaptable design will prove to be a better buy. Self-assembly bedroom furniture aimed at the younger market and made from hardwearing, easy-to-clean materials is versatile and inexpensive, and often offers desk space and storage in one package. A desk requires a comfortable chair but elsewhere children usually prefer to lounge, so squashy beanbags make excellent seating.

👍 **SAFETY TIP While children are very young, don't put beds or furniture too near a window. Fit windows with a locking stay or child safety lock so they can be opened slightly for ventilation but no further. You must avoid trailing flexes, do fit electrical sockets with safety covers and use a safety-stop to prevent doors slamming on tiny fingers.**

1

TOMMY'S FLOOR CHANGE

Carpets are never a good solution for children, it is much better to have a wipeable surface. Photographic floor tiles showing flowers (left), pebbles, grass or even water are available, These are easy to lay and might just please your fussy teenager.

STORAGE

As well as hanging and shelf space for clothes, storage is needed for toys and books that will rapidly grow in number as the child gets older.

Simple, low-level storage is most practical for younger children. Baskets and capacious crates that will slide under a bed or can be stacked against a wall are ideal, while colourful semi-transparent plastic crates allow the contents to be easily identified. Cube storage systems are also useful and adapt easily to changing needs. Try not to fill up most of the floor area, however, as this will still be the child's preferred play space.

From about the age of ten, toys start to make way for more sophisticated possessions and at this point you can also begin to make use of higher-level storage. Crates are still useful but appropriate containers will be needed for a proliferation of less bulky items. Remember that storage systems relevant to their interests and particularly those with an upbeat look – a state-of-the-art CD rack, jazzy box files or a professional make-up box – are more likely to get used than more mundane or childish options. If you are able to build a window seat into a child's room (see page 110), construct it with a lift-up lid for extra toy storage **1**.

PAINTING A CHALKBOARD

If you can give space on one of the bedroom walls over to a chalkboard, it offers a child the opportunity to express him or herself in words or drawing – or just to write cheeky messages!

First cut a circular mask out of sticky-backed film. For a perfect circle, pin one end of a length of string in the centre of the film and draw the outline with a pencil attached to the other end **2**. Cut out the shape using a craft knife on a board **3**. Then stick the outer circle in position on the wall **4** and mask off the area all around it with newspaper **5**, as the fine spray tends to spread far and wide.

Using special blackboard paint in an aerosol can, spray back and forth until you achieve a flat, even surface **6**, building up several layers. Leave it to dry overnight, after which time you (or your child!) can write on it with chalks.

soundproofing

Noise pollution is becoming an ever-present aspect of modern life. You may have reconciled yourself to the fact that unwelcome sounds may never go away, but they don't have to ruin your life – it is possible to find solutions by blocking or damping down excessive noise.

SOURCES OF NOISE

Noise from outside the house, like the roar of road traffic or the sound of trains or planes, can penetrate through gaps and cracks in the walls, as well as through doors, windows, floors, ceilings and roofs. Unwelcome noise from a neighbour, such as raised voices or a television set turned up to full volume, can be transmitted through party walls, even travelling up the wall to emerge on a different storey. For noise generated within the house, for example the high-decibel music played by teenagers, there are ways of both reducing the noise at source and reducing its transmission through the house. Each source of noise requires a different means of treatment, most of which have the added benefit of improving thermal insulation.

FILLING CRACKS AND GAPS

Start by making sure that you have fitted proper brush draught excluders to all windows and external doors **1**. There's a good choice of draught excluders available for front doors and all are easy to fit, needing only to be cut to size. The more expensive the excluder, the longer it will last. If you need to draughtproof an interior door, simple self-adhesive foam strip will make a big difference to the

noise that penetrates, but it will only last a year or two before needing replacement. Clean the door frame surface first, then just cut the foam to length with scissors, peel off the backing strip and stick it in place **2**. Draught excluding soon pays for

itself with reduced fuel bills coming through the post (remember to draughtproof the letterbox!).

If an interior door is allowing a draught underneath it, you could try lowering the door by repositioning the hinges so that the gap is at the top of the door rather than the bottom. But it is much easier to buy a door 'dog' and lay it across the door when it is closed.

Next, look at gaps around door and window frames and the external wall. Filling these gaps with mastic, applied with a caulking gun, will cut down noise as well as preventing the wood getting wet and rotting. Seal any holes where pipes or electric cable enter the house though an outside wall **3**.

SOUNDPROOFING DOORS

Too flimsy a front door is usually the culprit here – and the best answer is to replace the door with a thicker, more solid one. This will also improve security, especially if you fit the door with proper security locks.

If you can afford it, another possible solution for a front door is to add a porch. This has other benefits, including heat and draught reduction, in addition to cutting down considerably on noise from outside.

SOUNDPROOFING WINDOWS

Fitting heavier curtains with a good lining will help to cut down noise – but this will obviously be effective only when the curtains are drawn. For 24-hour noise reduction, fit double-glazing to your windows. The normal double-glazed replacement windows fitted to reduce heat loss will go some way towards reducing noise, but the reduction is most effective where you can allow a really large air gap (100–200mm/4–8in) between the two panes of glass.

Period properties, especially listed ones or those within conservation areas, have major problems arising from restrictions regarding double-glazed replacement windows. It is possible in some cases to fit purpose-made original-style wooden window frames designed to accept double-glazed glass units. Do NOT attempt to fit PVC windows into period properties, or you will be ordered to remove them!

SOUNDPROOFING FLOORS

A good thick carpet with a proper underlay is the best answer here, especially if you use one of the acoustic underlays or soundproofing mats available. More extreme measures involve laying a new floor on top of the existing floor, with insulating materials in between. The new floor should be tongue-and-groove floorboards, glued or clipped together but allowed to 'float' – they should not be nailed down to the existing floor. Since sound is transmitted from one floor to another through the floor and ceiling fixings to the joist, a floating floor eliminates the need for fixing the floor to these joists.

SOUNDPROOFING CEILINGS

You will do a lot to reduce the noise coming down from above if you have fitted proper loft insulation – the recommended thickness these days is 250mm (10in).

To stop noise coming down from an upstairs room, you can fit a false ceiling underneath the existing one. This is a major undertaking as it will involve making a framework to receive the plasterboard, strong enough to hold the new ceiling, but without reducing the height of the room too much (do not attach the new ceiling to the old one). You then cover the joists with plasterboard, adding insulating material between the joists (hold this in place with garden

4

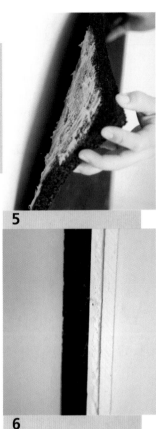

5

6

netting stapled to the joist sides). All this reduces the room height by a minimum of 150mm (6in). If this is not possible, you will need to go into the room above (provided it belongs to you!), lift the floorboards and add insulating material (acoustic mineral wool) between the joists. This will help to dampen the noise to some extent, but will not cure the problem

SOUNDPROOFING WALLS

The traditional method of soundproofing walls involves building a partition wall on the room side of the existing wall, putting insulating material (acoustic mineral wool) between the vertical studs and covering this with two layers of plasterboard. There should be a decent gap between the two walls, so this process reduces the room size by a minimum of 100mm (4in).

You can now buy soundproofing wall panels, which are easier to fit; they are simply stuck to the wall before being covered with two layers of plasterboard. Dab the adhesive supplied in the corners and at even spaces over each panel, and spread to form a thin layer over the whole area **4**. Fix each one to the prepared wall **5**, starting at the bottom corner and working across the bottom, then upwards. Leave to set overnight. Cut the plasterboard sheets to fit the wall and glue one at a time to the soundproof panels **6**. When the glue has set, skim plaster the wall to finish.

light solutions

Natural light is an essential component in creating a comfortable home – it opens up rooms, affects the way in which colours work together and helps to create a feeling of airy spaciousness. The amount of light in a room will, of course, be limited by the size of the windows and the direction the room faces, but with a little imagination it is possible to make much more of whatever light is available.

MAKING THE MOST OF DAYLIGHT

1

Where light is limited, the rule for windows is to keep it simple. Replace any light-absorbing voluminous drapes and heavy pelmets or valances with neat window blinds **1**, tailored curtains (tied well back during the day), or sheer voiles and muslins that will screen the glass without obliterating daylight.

2

If the view from a window is not essential, the glass can be sandblasted by a specialist glazier to create a classic etched effect that lets light through while still providing privacy. You can create your own etched glass more cheaply with self-adhesive glass film or by using a glass-frosting spray available from art shops and DIY stores **2**. The glass needs to be spotlessly clean and should be degreased with methylated spirit first. Simple designs can be created by masking the glass before applying the spray, while adhesive films are available in different patterns.

APPLYING SELF-ADHESIVE FILM
Thoroughly clean the window: go over the entire glass area with the scraper to remove all loose particles, fibres, paint spots and irregular putty lines, to produce a clean window with straight edges.

Clean the glass with methylated spirit **3**, then spray it with plenty of detergent solution **4**. Making sure you have

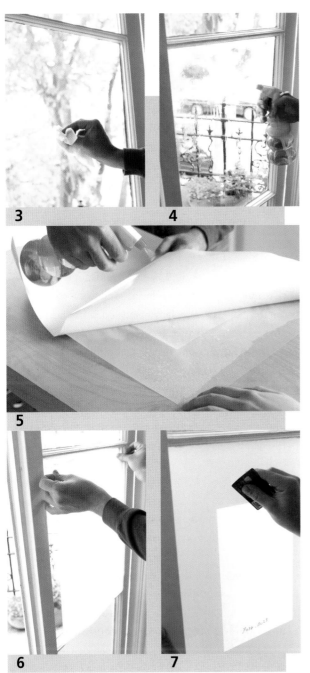

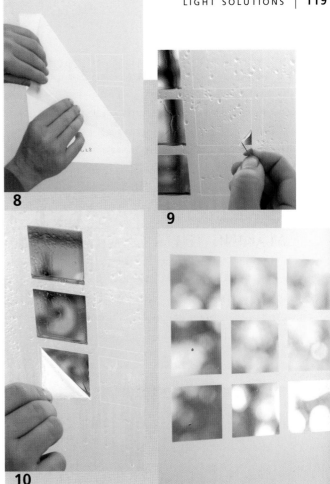

Holding the top two corners of the film with fingers and thumbs, gently offer the sticky side of the film to the window. Position and lightly press it into place **6**.

With the film in the correct position, starting from the centre, carefully remove the detergent solution and any bubbles by running a credit card over the film **7**. Check from the outside that all bubbles are removed. If not, run over the film again.

Leave the film in place for 3–4 hours, then carefully remove the carry tape protecting the cut-out shapes **8**. (The film may lift off slightly, but can be smoothed back in place with the credit card, once the carry tape is removed.)

With a pin, pick out the relevant shapes **9**, and peel off the film **10**. Run over the film and cut-out edges again with the credit card. Finally, check the exterior for any air bubbles and smooth out again if necessary. The film should be thoroughly 'fixed' after about 24 hours.

clean hands, lay the film, face down, on a clean, flat, dust-free surface.

You will need someone to help you with the next step. Carefully peel off the backing paper, spraying the sticky surface generously with plenty of detergent solution (using a fine spray) while your assistant holds the top two corners of the film **5**. You can touch the sticky side when it is wet, but only very sparingly.

WALLS

The imaginative use of glass indoors can dramatically affect the apparent proportions of a room and the amount of light available. Replacing a non-load-bearing wall or creating a partition with glass bricks will allow diffused light to filter from one room to the next **1**, while still offering an element of privacy. Glass bricks also make a stunning but practical material for constructing a shower enclosure. Their semi-industrial look complements that of contemporary interiors; they are available in a limited number of colours as well as clear.

A window set into an internal wall will brighten a gloomy corner by borrowing light from an adjoining room and a non-loading-bearing wall or stud partition offers the perfect opportunity to create a vista between one room and the next. Wooden window frames with a slim profile in a circular, oval or arched shape look best used like this.

1

QUICK TRICKS

Using mirrors is a quick and easy way to reflect light and create the illusion of space. One large mirror will double the perceived space in a small room by increasing the light and giving the room depth via a reflected image. For good light distribution, the best places to hang a mirror are directly opposite or, in a long room, at right angles to the window. Using mirrors all along one wall will bounce light the full length of a long, narrow hallway.

DECORATION

Pale colours reflect up to 80 per cent of light while dark colours absorb nearly 90 per cent, so if you want to maximise the sense of light and space, decorating with gentle colours is essential. Using light-reflective finishes will also help to magnify and distribute light around a room (see pages 40–43). Light-reflective finishes include high-gloss paints and silk vinyl emulsion, wallcoverings with a sheen, and glazed ceramic or metallic tiles. Metal-framed furniture, polished wood and leather, glass, any surface with a lustre and even satinized fabrics, all have light-reflecting potential.

DOORS

Doors are another way to introduce glass and therefore more light into the home. External glass doors **2** offer not just light but the feeling of bringing the outside indoors, extending your space. Internal glass doors offer privacy without blocking out light and create a sense of continuity from room to room. They are particularly useful for dividing a large room into two, and opening up small spaces where solid doors would make the room seem claustrophobic. A hardwood door with a double-glazed panel is a good compromise between providing security and allowing light into a gloomy hall.

It is possible to replace wooden panels in existing doors with toughened safety glass, but do cost out the job first. Pre-glazed internal doors are available at competitive prices from DIY superstores and it may be cheaper simply to replace the doors rather than incur the expense of having glazing made-to-measure – unless, of course, it's a period property or your doors are of superb quality!

2

3

ROOF WINDOWS

Provide extra light in a gloomy extension by installing a window in the roof **3** and **4**. Rooflights are designed for a roof pitch greater than 20 degrees and can be fitted from the inside. They admit up to 40 per cent more light than a conventional window of the same size and can be operated manually or by remote control. Modern roof domes are for flat roofs or roofs with a shallow pitch, up to 15 degrees. They come in a range of light-catching designs.

If you have a dark hallway or stairwell, it may be possible to introduce light from outside via a 'light pipe' fitted to the roof through an upstairs ceiling **5**. These work by clever use of mirrors and glass and can be very effective. The most suitable place for a light pipe is on a south-facing roof slope, located as near to the ridge as possible. In most homes, light pipes will fit between existing rafters or joists. However, if there isn't enough space, one rafter and ceiling joist may be cut to allow the installation – provided you clear this with a structural engineer.

Light pipes are not much bigger than a flue pipe or a chimney and, unless you are in a conservation area, you do not need planning permission. It is possible to buy a kit to assemble a light pipe yourself, but since it involves going up on to a pitched roof, the job is better left to a professional, who may need to erect a tower or scaffold. If

4

you have a loft, determine first where you want the light pipe to come into the loft from below and where you want it to exit through the roof. Make sure there are no obstructions, such as water tanks or cables.

5

There is no limit to the number of lengths or bends that you use, but each pipe length loses approximately 10 per cent and for each 2-section bend approximately 16 per cent light is lost. The suggested maximum length of the light pipe is 10m (33ft) and up to five 2-section bends.

glossary

Airlock A blockage in a pipe caused by a trapped air bubble.

Appliance Any machine or device that is powered by electricity.

Architrave The moulding around a window or door.

Back-siphoning Siphoning of part of a plumbing system due to the mains water pressure failing.

Baluster One of a set of posts supporting a stair handrail.

Balustrade The protective barrier alongside a staircase or landing.

Base coat A flat coat of paint over which a layer of glaze is applied.

Batten A narrow strip of wood, usually fixed to a wall to act as a support for a unit or shelving.

Bevel Any angle at which two pieces of wood meet, other than a right angle.

Bore The hollow part of a pipe.

Butt joint A simple joint where two pieces of wood are fixed together with no interlocking parts cut in them.

Cap-nut A nut used to tighten a fitting onto pipework.

Cavity wall A wall made of two separate, parallel masonry skins with an air space between.

Chamfer A flat, narrow surface along the edge of a workpiece, usually at a 45° angle to any adjacent surfaces.

Chase A groove cut in masonry or plaster for electrical cabling or pipework.

Circuit A complete path through which an electric current flows.

Concave Curving inwards.

Conductor A component, usually a length of wire, along which an electric current will pass.

Consumer unit The box containing all the fuse ways that protect the individual circuits in the house. The main on-off switch is located here, enabling you to isolate the power supply to the whole house.

Convex Curving outwards.

Cornice A continuous horizontal moulding between walls and ceiling.

Counterbore A tapered recess that allows the head of a screw or bolt to lie below a surface; also to cut such a recess.

Countersink To cut a tapered recess that allows the head of a screw or bolt to lie flush with a surface.

Cup To bend as a result of shrinkage; usually referred to as across the length of a piece of wood.

Dado The lower part of an interior wall – usually a moulded wooden rail at waist height.

Damp-proof course (DPC) A layer of impervious material that prevents moisture rising through a floor or in a wall.

Earth A connection between the earth or ground and an electrical circuit; also a terminal to which this connection is made.

Extension lead A length of electrical flex for the temporary connection of an appliance to a wall socket.

Face edge A woodworking term for a surface that is planed square to the face side (see below).

Face side A woodworking term for a flat, planed surface from which other angles and dimensions are measured and worked.

Fence An adjustable guide to keep the cutting edge of a tool a set distance from the edge of a workpiece.

Four-way A block of four electrical sockets connected to a wall socket by an extension lead.

Free-standing Furniture or units that are not built-in or fixed to a wall or floor.

Fuse board A unit where a main electrical service cable is connected to the circuits in a house; also a term covering a meter, consumer unit, etc.

Galvanized Covered with a protective coating of zinc.

Grain The direction of wood fibres in a particular workpiece; also a pattern on the surface of timber made by cutting through the fibres.

Groove A long, narrow channel cut in plaster or wood; in the latter, this follows the direction of the grain.

Grounds Strips of wood fixed to a wall to provide nail-fixing points for skirting boards, etc.

Housing A long, narrow channel cut across the general direction of wood grain to form part of a joint.

Insulation Material used to reduce the transmission of heat or sound; also a non-conductive material around electrical wires or connections to prevent the passage of electricity.

Isolating valve A valve used to shut off water from a particular room or appliance, so as not to have to turn off the entire water system.

Joist A horizontal wooden or metal beam (such as a RSJ) used to support a structure such as a floor, ceiling or wall.

Key To roughen a surface to provide a better grip when it is being glued; also the surface so roughened.

Knotting Sealer, made from shellac, that prevents wood resin bleeding through a surface finish.

Knurled On a knob or handle, a series of fine grooves impressed into an edge or surface to improve the grip when turned or handled.

Laminate Two or more sheets of material bonded together; or the top waterproof sheet of the bonded sheets used as a work surface; also to fix such sheets together.

Lintel A horizontal beam used to support the wall over a door or window opening.

Lipping A decorative strip applied to the side edges of laminated boards.

MDF Medium-density fibreboard, a man-made sheet material that can be worked like wood and is used as a substitute for it.

Mitre A joint between two pieces of wood formed by cutting 45° bevels at the end of each piece; also to cut such a joint.

Noggin Horizontal reinforcing timber fixed between the vertical studs in a stud partition wall.

Pilot hole A small-diameter hole drilled to act as a guide for a screw thread.

Primer A coat of paint applied to wood or metal to seal it and act as a first coat.

Profile The outline or contour of an object.

PTFE tape Tape made from polytetrafluorethylene, used to seal threaded plumbing fittings.

RCD Residual circuit device, a device that monitors the flow of electrical current through the live and neutral wires of a circuit.

Rebate A stepped rectangular recess along the edge of a workpiece, usually forming part of a joint; also to cut such a recess.

Reveal The vertical side of an opening.

Rising main A pipe that supplies water under mains pressure, usually to a roof storage tank.

Score To scratch a line with a pointed tool.

Scribe To copy the profile of a surface on the edge of sheet material to be butted against it; also to mark a line with a pointed tool.

Sheathing An outer layer of insulation on an electrical cable or flex.

Short circuit Accidental re-routing of electricity to earth, which increases the flow of current and consequently blows a fuse.

Silicone mastic A non-setting compound used to seal joints.

Spur Branch cable that extends an existing electrical circuit.

Stud partition A timber frame interior dividing wall.

Template A cut-out pattern, made from paper, wood, metal etc, used to help shape a workpiece accurately.

Terminal A connection to which bared ends of electrical cable or flex are attached.

Trap A bent section of pipe below a bath, sink, etc., containing standing water to prevent the passage of gases.

U-bend A waste pipe, or part of one, shaped like a U, used as part of a trap.

Undercoat A layer or layers of paint used to cover primer and build up a protective layer before a top coat is applied.

index

suppliers

DECORATING

AKZONOBEL INTERNATIONAL
floor and radiator paint
tel: 01480 484 284
web: www.international-paints.co.uk

CROWN
paint suppliers
tel: 0870 240 1127 paint talk helpline
web: www.crownpaint.co.uk

CWV GROUP (CROWN WALLCOVERINGS)
wallpaper and textiles suppliers
tel: 0800 458 1554 general enquiries
web: www.cwvgroup.com

HARRIS
painting and decorating tools
tel: 24 hour freephone order line 0800 136 982
email: sales@lgharris.co.uk
web: www.lgharris.co.uk

HENKEL
DIY products (solvite, unibond, nitromors)
tel: 01707 289 000 general enquiries
web: www.makingdiyeasier.co.uk

PALACE CHEMICALS
Peel-Away paint stripper
tel: 0151 486 6101 technical service line
email: sales@palacechemicals.co.uk
web: www.palacechemicals.co.uk

PLASTI-KOTE
spray paints, perfect finish fast
tel: 01223 836 400 for stockists
web: www.plasti-kote.com
web: www.spraypaint.co.uk

RONSEAL
interior and exterior wood care supplier
tel: 0114 240 9469 technical & product
email: enquiry@ronseal.co.uk
web: www.ronseal.co.uk

FLOORING

BRINTONS
manufacturers of high quality woven carpets
tel: 0800 50 50 55 consumer helpline
email: samples@brintons.co.uk
web: www.brintons.net

DALSOUPLE
rubber flooring suppliers
tel: 01278 727 733 for stockists
email: info@dalsouple.com
web: www.dalsouple.com

FIRED EARTH
flooring, furniture and fabrics
tel: 01295 814 300 for stockists
email: enquiries@firedearth.com
web: www.firedearth.com

HARVEY MARIA
photographic vinyl flooring
tel: 020 8542 0088

email: info@harveymaria.co.uk
web: www.harveymaria.co.uk

ROGER OATES
specialists in runners for halls and stairs
tel: 01531 631 611 head office
email: sales@rogeroates.com
web: www.rogeroates.com

SOLID FLOOR
solid timber flooring
tel: 020 7221 9166 or through website
email: info@solidfloor.co.uk
web: www.solidfloor.co.uk

THE CARPET STORE
for all your flooring needs
tel: 020 8749 9340

VICTORIAN WOODWORKS
hardwood flooring
tel: 020 8534 1000
email: sales@victorianwoodworks.co.uk
web: www.victorianwoodworks.co.uk

YARD OF INTEREST
reclaimed floorboards and other materials
tel: 020 8995 7171

FURNITURE

CADIRA
contemporary furniture
tel: 08700 414 180
email: info@cadira.co.uk
web: www.cadira.co.uk

GAUTIER
contemporary furniture
tel: 01727 877 977 general enquiries
email: enquiries@gautier.co.uk
web: www.gautier.fr

HIDEAWAY BEDS
foldaway/hideaway beds
tel: 01752 51 11 11 general enquiries
email: info@hideaway.co.uk
web: www.hideaway.co.uk

IKEA
furniture & accessories suppliers
tel: 0845 355 1141 for stockists
email: via website
web: www.ikea.co.uk for stock availability

STANLEY HOME SOLUTIONS
sliding door walk-in wardrobes
tel: 08701 650 650
web: www.stanleyworks.com

OTHER SUPPLIERS

B&Q
major DIY store for everything you need
tel: 0845 222 1000
web: www.diy.com

BAL
tile cleaner suppliers
tel: 01782 591 160 customer services
email: info@building-adhesives.com
web: www.building-adhesives.com

CUSTOM AUDIO DESIGN
DIY soundproofing products
tel: 0870 747 5432 for customer service
email: sales@customaudiodesigns.co.uk
web: www.nonoise.co.uk

HIB (HOME IMPROVEMENT BUREAU
mirror mosaic
tel: 020 8 441 0352 customer services
email: sales@hib.co.uk
web: www.hib.co.uk

JEWSON
building supplies
tel: 0800 539 766
email: customer.services@jewson.co.uk
web: www.jewson.co.uk

MK ELECTRIC
electrical suppliers
tel: mk helpline 0870 240 3385
web: www.mkelectric.co.uk

MONODRAUGHT
natural lighting and ventilation
tel: 0845 201 2555
email: info@monodraught.com
web: www.sunpipe.com

THE FIREPLACE SHOP
specializing in traditional fireplaces
tel: 020 8741 5013 general enquiries
web: www.the-fireplace-shop.co.uk

THE HOLDING COMPANY
storage organisation
tel: 020 8445 2888 mail order
email: admin@theholdingcompany.co.u
web: www.theholdingcompany.co.uk

THINK PICTURES
framed pictures
tel: 01273 513 876
web: www.thinkpictures.co.uk

TOOLS

ATLAS COPCO (brand name Milwauke
power tool suppliers
tel: 01442 222 378 for nearest dealer
email: milwaukee@uk.atlascopco.com
web: www.milwaukee_et.com

BLACK & DECKER
power tool suppliers
tel: 01753 511 234 for customer helplin
email: info@blackanddecker.co.uk
web: www.blackanddecker.co.uk

DE WALT
power tool suppliers
tel: 0700 433 9258 for stockists
email: via website
web: www.dewalt.co.uk

MARSHALLTOWN & ESTWING TOO
power tool suppliers (supplied by Rollins
email: sales@rollins.co.uk
web: www.rollins.co.uk

SCREWFIX DIRECT
tool suppliers

tel: 0500 414 141
email: online@screwfix.com
web: www.screwfix.com

STANLEY
hand tools suppliers
tel: 08701 650 650
web: www.stanleyworks.com

WINDOWS
BRADLEY COLLECTION
curtain accessories
tel: 08451 187 224 for customer services

email: info@bradleycollection.co.uk
web: www.bradleycollection.co.uk

BRUME
window film
tel: 0136 473 951brochure request line
email: info@brume.co.uk
web: www.brume.co.uk

ECLECTICS
made-to-measure blinds
tel: 0870 010 2211 for brochures
web: www.eclectics.co.uk

LUXAFLEX
made-to-measure blinds
tel: 0800 652 7799 for stockists
web: www.luxaflex.com

THE NEW ENGLAND SHUTTER CO.
bespoke shutters
tel: 0208 675 1099
email: sales@tnesc.co.uk
web: www.tnesc.co.uk

photography credits

2–5 All David Murphy; **7–12** All Mike Newton, (b) Sarah Cuttle;
13 David Murphy; **14–15** All Sarah Cuttle (br), David Murphy;
16–17 (1–2) AWs David Ashby, (3–9) David Murphy/MK Electrics;
18–19 AWs David Ashby, (1–6) David Murphy/MK Electrics; **20–23**
All Sarah Cuttle, (br) Ikea); **24–25** All Sarah Cuttle (br) Shuttercraft;
26–27 All Sarah Cuttle; **28–29** All Sarah Cuttle, (4) David Murphy;
30–31 All David Murphy, (7–10) Sarah Cuttle; **32** All Sarah Cuttle;
33–35 All David Murphy; **36** All David Murphy (5) Artex Warlplug;
37–39 All David Murphy; **42–43** (1) The Loft Shop, (2–4) Crown,
(br) CWV Group; **44–49** All David Murphy, (except bl p.49 CWV
Group); **50–52** All Sarah Cuttle, except br p.51, Crown; **53–55** All
David Murphy; **56–57** (1) CWV Group, (2) EASIpanel (SPAtec),
(3) Victorian Woodworks, (4–5) Fired Earth; **58–59** (1) Crown
(2) Brintons (3) Fired earth (4) Victorian Woodworks, (5) CWV
Group (6) The Holding Company: **60–61** (1) Richard Burbridge,
(2) Valor/The Baxi Group, (3) Richard Burbridge, (4) Crown,
(5) Eclectics; **62–63** (1) Victorian Woodworks, (2) Brintons, (3) CWV
group, (4–5) Shuttercraft, (6) Ikea, (7) Cadira; **64–65** (1) Fired Earth,
(2) Luxaflex, (3) Gautier, (4) Dulux, (5) Fired Earth, (6) Crown;
66–67 (1) Hammonds, (2) Gautier, (3) Ikea, (4) The Holding
Company, (5) Brintons, (6) John Cullen Lighting; **68–69** (1) Crown,
(2) B&Q, (3) Ikea, (4) B&Q; **70–71** (1) Sharps Home Office, (2) Spur
Shelving, (3) The Cotswold Company, (4) Sharps Home Office,
(5) Hammonds Home Offices; **72** (1) B&Q, (2) Brintons, (3) Sharps
Home Office; **73** David Murphy; **74–75** All David Murphy (br) Roger
Oates; **76–77** All David Murphy/B&Q, (bl) B&Q; **78–79** (1) BAL
(2–10) All David Murphy; **80–83** All David Murphy (A) Ronseal,
(B) Akzonobel, (br) Ronseal; **84–85** All David Murphy; **86** (bl) Fired
Earth, (tr), Valor/The Baxi Group; **87–89** All David Murphy (bl 88)
Think Pictures; **90–91** (1) Fired Earth (2–5) Sarah Cuttle, (tr), Fired
Earth, (br) all David Murphy; **92–93** (1–2) Bradley Collection,
(3–4) Crown, (5) Fired Earth, (6) CWV Group, (7) Russlette; **94–95**
(1) Eclectics, (2) Gautier, (3–5) Luxaflex, (br) David Murphy; **96–97**
All David Murphy/The Shutter Company; **98–99** All David Murphy;
100–101 (1–2) Hideaway Beds, (3–5) David Murphy/Hideaway
Beds; **102–105** All Sarah Cuttle; **106–107** (6–8) Sarah Cuttle/
Stanley, (bl) Stanley, (9) Gautier, (10) Sarah Cuttle, (br) all Gautier;
108–109 (1) Cadira, (2) Gautier, (tr) Spur Shelving, (3) Ikea, (4) The
Holding Company, (5) Gautier; **110–113** All David Murphy;
114–115 (1) David Murphy, (2–6) Sarah Cuttle/Plasti-Kote; **116–117**
(1–3) David Murphy, (4–6) David Murphy/Custom Audio Designs;
118–119 (1) B&Q, (2) David Murphy/Plasti-Kote, (3–10) David
Murphy/Brume; **120–121** (1) Amanda Jensen, (2–3) Fired Earth, (4)
Ikea, (5) Monodraught

acknowledgements

TOMMY'S
*An enormous thanks to my wife Marie for having to type up every
word of my often illegible scribble onto the PC.*
*Georgie Bennett, Richard Foy, Micky Cunningham and Jimmy the
Joiner for vital information!*
*To Ruth, Angela, Amanda, Alastair, David, Hannah, Sarah, Anthony,
Antony, Neal, Andres, Max and Sarah C. for their help and patience
in co-ordinating and stitching together this book!*
*And a special thanks to my old friends Guy and Sarah at B&Q for
all their help supplying goods for this book. And a big thank you to
Jane Fielding for letting me mend her encaustic tile floor*

FOR AIREDALE PUBLISHING
We would like to thank the following companies for providing
tools and equipment for this book:
FOR EVERYTHING FROM A–Z
Guy Burtenshaw, Sarah Stonebanks at B&Q
and all the very patient staff at B&Q *Yeading*
and thank you Trevor and Simon at Screwfix
FOR EVERYTHING ELSE
Karen Lees at Hideaway *for the swing-away bed*
Angela Turner and Anika Birchall for the Stanley *Wardrobe*
Nick Dudley-Williams for the Stanley *Tools*
Matthew Page at Harris *for all painting and wallpapering
equipment*
Julie Doyle and Dan Turner at ICAS *for Crown paint and MK
Electrics for the consumer unit and new sockets*
John Armstrong at Ronseal *for woodfloor products*
Ruth Weir for Henkel *products – Solvite, Unibond, Nitromors*
Anna Hollingsworth at Plasti-Kote *for all the spray products*
Mark Findlay at Harvey Maria *for the photographic vinyl tiles*
Tom Sykes at Custom Audio Designs *for the sound insulation sheet*
Beverley Mills and Karen Landsdown for the Brume *window film*
Steven Kaye at The Home Improvement Bureau *for mirror mosaic*
Kay Porter and Marianne Wolff at BAL *for tile cleaning products*
George Zacal at the CWV Group *for wallpaper*
Eelke Jan Bles at Solid Floor *for solid wood flooring*
Polly Noble for Roger Oates *stair runners and carpet*
Simon Eadit at The New England Shutter Company
Colin Williams at Palace Chemicals *for Peel-Away paint stripper*